PROJECTILE SCIENCE

The Physics Behind Kicking a Field Goal and Launching a Rocket with Science Activities for Kids

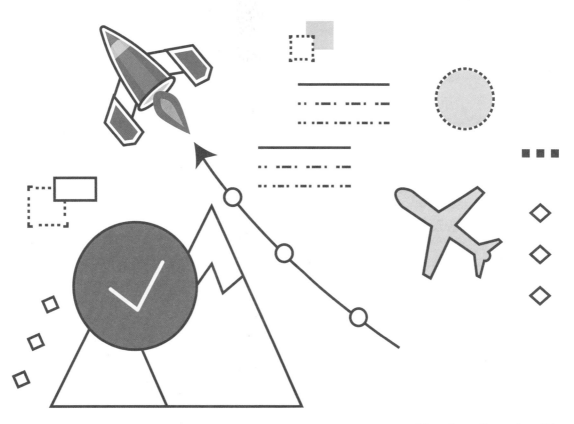

Matthew Brenden Wood

Illustrated by Tom Casteel

Titles in the **Technology Today** book set

  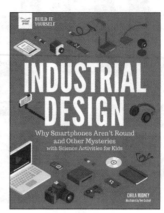 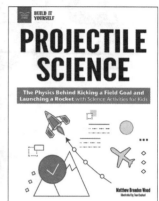

Check out more titles at www.nomadpress.net

Nomad Press
A division of Nomad Communications
10 9 8 7 6 5 4 3 2 1

This book was manufactured by Friesens Book Division
Altona, MB, Canada
August 2018, Job #244131

ISBN Softcover: 978-1-61930-678-3
ISBN Hardcover: 978-1-61930-676-9

Educational Consultant, Marla Conn

Questions regarding the ordering of this book should be addressed to
Nomad Press
2456 Christian St.
White River Junction, VT 05001
www.nomadpress.net

Printed in Canada.

Contents

Interested in Primary Sources?

Look for this icon. Use a smartphone or tablet app to scan the QR code and explore more! Photos are also primary sources because a photograph takes a picture at the moment something happens.

If the QR code doesn't work, there's a list of URLs on the Resources page. Or, try searching the internet with the Keyword Prompts to find other helpful sources.

🔎 projectiles

1304 CE: King Edward of England uses a giant trebuchet known as the "Wolf of War" to help conquer Stirling Castle in Scotland.

1337 CE: The English longbow is used in the Hundred Years' War between England and France.

1346 CE: The Mongol army uses catapults to infect the city of Caffa with bubonic plague.

1415 CE: At the Battle of Agincourt, English forces use longbows to defeat a French army nearly 10 times larger.

1520 CE: Gun barrels are first made with spiral grooves that spin projectiles, called "rifles."

1638 CE: Galileo Galilei shows that the motion of a projectile is a curved path called a parabola.

1812 CE: The British Navy uses rockets to attack Fort McHenry, inspiring Francis Scott Key to write the words "the rocket's red glare."

1846 CE: Isaac Newton's law of universal gravitation is used to discover the planet Neptune.

1849 CE: Claude-Etienne Minié invents the modern, streamlined bullet.

c. 1850 CE: The first slingshots using rubber are made.

1853 CE: German physicist H.G. Magnus describes how spinning objects curve in flight.

c. 1853 CE: Scottish physicist William Rankine coins the term "potential energy."

October 7, 1867: William Arthur "Candy" Cummings throws the first curveball in a baseball game.

1905: Pitcher Eddie Cicotte earns the nickname "knuckles" for the strange grip he uses for a pitch that seems to zig and zag on its way to the plate.

September 5, 1906: Bradbury Robinson throws the first spiral pass in American football.

March 16, 1926: The first liquid-fueled rocket is launched by Robert Goddard.

September 8, 1944: The first V2 rocket attack happens on London, England.

1953: The Wiffle ball is invented.

1959: Engineer and physicist Lyman Briggs proves that a curveball really curves.

October 4, 1957: *Sputnik* becomes the world's first artificial satellite.

February 9, 1959: The Soviet Union's R-7 becomes the world's first operational intercontinental ballistic missile (ICBM).

April 12, 1961: Cosmonaut Yuri Gagarin, riding on top of a Soviet R-7 ICBM, becomes the first human in space.

May 5, 1961: Alan Shepard becomes the first American in space.

1966: Hollis Wilbur Allen builds the first compound bow.

November 9, 1967: The first launch of the Saturn V, the rocket that took humans to the moon.

September 8, 1974: Daredevil Robert "Evel" Knievel jumps across the Snake River Canyon in his custom-built "Skycycle X-2."

June 2, 1987: Joey Meyer of the Denver Zephyrs hits a 582-foot home run, probably the longest home run in baseball history.

2009: The game Angry Birds uses projectile science to enterain humans for hours.

2010: The U.S. Navy fires the fastest projectile ever, traveling at more than 8,000 feet per second.

2011: "Chucky III" sets the world record for catapult distance, flinging a pumpkin 3,636 feet.

December 8, 2013: Matt Prater of the Denver Broncos kicks the longest field goal in NFL history—64 yards!

THE SCIENCE OF
PROJECTILES

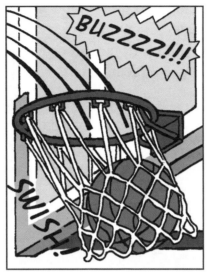

Down by a point with only seconds left in the game, you square up your shoulders to take the final shot. Over the outstretched hands of the defender, you release the basketball and watch as it soars through the air into the hoop with a swoosh. The buzzer sounds and the crowd cheers—you've won the game!

You might think that nailing a three-pointer is just luck. There are many **forces** at work, however, that determine if you've made a game-winning shot or the final out.

If you've ever thrown a ball, launched a model rocket, or even played video games, you've explored the amazing world of **ballistics**. Ballistics is the study of **projectiles** and of **projectile motion**—or how objects such as bullets and baseballs move. The study of **projectile science** can involve something as simple as tossing a soda can into a recycling bin from across the room or as complicated as sending a rocket into outer space. If it can be launched, thrown, fired, or flung, it's a projectile!

ESSENTIAL QUESTION

Why did ancient humans develop methods of sending projectiles farther, faster? How did this ability make life better?

WORDS TO KNOW

force: a push or pull applied to an object.

ballistics: the science that studies the movement of objects that are shot through the air.

projectile: an object that is thrown or launched and does not move by its own power.

projectile motion: the path that a projectile takes as it travels.

projectile science: the study of how projectiles move.

buoyancy: the force that makes something able to float, either in the air or in the water.

prehistoric: having to do with ancient times, before written human records.

tundra: a treeless Arctic region that is permanently frozen below the top layer of soil.

prey: an animal caught or hunted for food.

wary: suspicious.

lance: a long, straight wooden spear.

spear: a weapon with a long shaft and pointed tip, used for thrusting or throwing.

All projectiles follow the same rules of motion, no matter what they are. Understanding those rules is the science of ballistics. How hard do you need to throw a football to complete a pass? How do you aim an arrow to hit a bulls-eye? All these things require an understanding of ballistics and projectile motion.

If you think about it, you've been studying ballistics your whole life without knowing it! But to people throughout history, the study of ballistics was an even more important part of their lives.

Projectile or Not?

When is an object a projectile? Not all things flying through the air are projectiles! Projectiles don't move under their own power. Therefore, airplanes, helicopters, and hot air balloons are not projectiles because they use wings, engines, or **buoyancy** to determine how they move.

ANCIENT PROJECTILES

Imagine you're a **prehistoric** human, living with your prehistoric family in the harsh **tundra** of northern Siberia 20,000 years ago. Survival isn't easy! You must hunt large and dangerous beasts to provide for your family. But getting close to a bear or giant woolly mammoth is difficult. How do you hunt a fearsome animal without putting yourself in danger?

Ancient humans painting images of woolly mammoths on cave walls
credit: Charles R. Knight

Ancient people around the world solved this problem by using projectiles. Many used rounded stones as weapons, hurling them with great force to stun or knock down their **prey**. Others made slings, which allowed them to throw rocks with even greater force. Using projectiles to hunt had two big advantages for ancient people—it allowed them to sneak up on **wary** prey, and it kept them away from dangerous teeth and tusks.

An even more dangerous weapon made by ancient people was the **lance**, or **spear**. The first spears were simple, sharp sticks that could be thrown. People learned pretty quickly that attaching a small, sharpened rock to the tip made spears more accurate—and even more deadly.

WORDS TO KNOW

catapult: a large war machine used to hurl objects at an enemy.

Middle Ages: the period of European history after the fall of the Roman Empire, from about 350 to 1450 CE.

trebuchet: a large, catapult-like structure with a moveable arm that launched damaging items into or over castle walls.

siege: surrounding and attacking a fortified place, such as a fort, and cutting it off from help and supplies.

siege engine: a machine built to help forces break through walls—or go over them.

culture: the beliefs and way of life of a group of people, which can include religion, language, art, clothing, food, holidays, tools, and more.

fire lance: a very early gunpowder weapon.

Hurling spears worked well, but you still needed to be pretty close to your prey. A new tool, the bow and arrow, gave hunters an even better way to hunt from afar. For the first archers, making bows and arrows was much harder than fashioning a spear. They needed to find the right kind of wood to make a bow—something that could bend but not break. Plant and animal materials were needed to make the bow string, and the arrows needed to be shaped and carved as straight as possible.

Finding all the right materials and creating the bows and arrows would have been difficult, but worth it. A well-made bow and arrow is much easier to aim than a spear. It's also lighter and easier to carry.

Projectiles were terrific for hunting food more easily and more efficiently. They were also used in battle.

ANCIENT WEAPONS

Have you ever seen a **catapult**? During the **Middle Ages**, catapults were used to send boulders over castle walls or even break them down. Catapults work a lot like a bow. A flexible piece of wood is pulled back into a firing position and loaded with a projectile. When it's released, the wood springs back, hurling the boulder at its target.

Trebuchets were another kind of catapult used in ancient warfare. Trebuchets used a large weight to send heavy objects flying. These **siege engines** dominated battlefields for hundreds of years until a new invention replaced them—firearms.

In the tenth century, a new kind of weapon was invented in China. The **fire lance** was a hollow bamboo tube filled with black powder and attached to the end of a spear. When it was lit, the black-powder exploded, sending fire and small projectiles toward the enemy.

DID YOU KNOW?

Bows, spears and other tools were invented by diverse **cultures** in different ways. The earliest evidence of archery comes from projectile points that are nearly 70,000 years old and found in South African caves. In Europe, the oldest bows and arrows are about 15,000 years old.

SAFETY FIRST

While you're building, exploring, and experimenting, remember to be safe. When working with projectiles, **ALWAYS** wear eye protection. Never point a projectile at something you don't want to hunt or damage, including people, pets, and valuable items. As you build and experiment, remember that things can pinch, snap, and even break, so be careful of your fingers and hands. Always practice safe science!

WORDS TO KNOW

physics: the study of physical forces, including matter, energy, and motion, and how these forces interact with each other.

air resistance: the force that acts on an object as it travels through the air.

spear-thrower: a stick that makes it possible to throw spears farther and faster.

prototype: a model of something that allows engineers to test their idea.

Eventually, the bamboo tube was replaced by a metal tube. A single projectile—the first bullet—was put inside. Loaded with gunpowder, the weapon was more powerful than a bow and deadlier than an arrow. Cannons, mortars, and modern rifles came later, firing larger projectiles even greater distances.

In 1961, Yuri Gagarin (1934–1968) became the first person to go into space, riding atop a ballistic missile that followed the same basic laws as basketballs and bullets. How does it work? What's behind the motion projectiles make once they leave your hand or shoot out of a device?

Projectile Science: The Physics Behind Kicking a Field Goal and Launching a Rocket examines the ups and downs of projectile motion by exploring the math and **physics** behind hitting the bulls-eye and reaching orbit. Along the way, you'll conduct experiments and safely build your own devices, such as slingshots, catapults, and water rockets.

You'll learn how to predict the paths of objects, including how far they'll fly and where they'll land. You'll also discover how things such as **air resistance** and spin can affect the flight of projectiles, including how curveballs curve and how bullets can be so accurate. Ballistics is an exciting way to explore the math and physics behind projectile motion!

Heads Up!

Many cultures created a tool to help throw spears farther and faster. Called an "atlatl" by the Aztecs and "woomera" by aboriginal Australians, a **spear-thrower** acts like an extension of the hunter's arm, giving greater power and accuracy.

You can watch modern people using ancient throwing tools in this video.

🔎 spear thrower Ice Age

Engineering Design Process

Every engineer keeps a notebook to keep track of their ideas and their steps in the engineering design process. As you read through this book and do the activities, keep track of your observations, data, and designs in an engineering design worksheet, like the one shown here. When doing an activity, remember that there is no right answer or right way to approach a project. Be creative and have fun!

Problem: What problem are we trying to solve?
Research: Has anything been invented to help solve the problem? What can we learn?
Question: Are there any special requirements for the device? An example of this is a car that must go a certain distance in a certain amount of time.
Brainstorm: Draw lots of designs for your device and list the materials you are using!
Prototype: Build the design you drew during brainstorming.
Test: Test your **prototype** and record your observations.
Evaluate: Analyze your test results. Do you need to make adjustments? Do you need to try a different prototype?

Each chapter of this book begins with an essential question to help guide your exploration of ballistics. Keep the question in your mind as you read the chapter. At the end of each chapter, use your engineering notebook to record your thoughts and answers.

ESSENTIAL QUESTION

Why did ancient humans develop methods of sending projectiles farther, faster? How did this ability make life better?

FIND PROJECTILES AROUND YOU

Projectiles can be almost anything—a ball, an arrow, and a bullet are all examples. While these are very different objects, do they move the same?

❯ **Observe the motion of several different projectiles you can find around you.** They can be a ball, stone, arrow—anything that can be safely thrown.

* What does it take to get the objects moving? Can you throw it or kick it? Does it need a device to move? Remember to practice safe science. Never point a projectile at something you don't want to hurt, including people, pets, and valuable items.

* What are the motions of your projectiles like? How are they alike and how are they different?

* What brings them to a halt? Are they fired at a target or do they simply land on the ground? What do you think happens when the objects stop moving?

Try This!

Play *Angry Birds* online! Using a slingshot, you can hurl birds, which are the projectiles, and follow their paths to the target. What do you notice about the motion of the projectiles in *Angry Birds*? Record your observations. How does changing the angle of the launch change the flight of projectiles? How does changing the stretch of the slingshot change the path of a bird? What is more important, the angle or how fast the bird flies?

🔎 play
Angry Birds

Chapter 1

WHAT GOES UP:
THE LAWS OF MOTION

Have you ever thought about what really happens when you throw a ball or fire a slingshot? What gets projectiles moving? And what brings them to a stop? You know that a baseball doesn't just send itself flying over the outfield fence, a golf ball won't move until it's struck by a club, and a soda can won't toss itself into a recycling container. For anything to move, a force needs to be applied. So let's get moving!

A force can be something simple, such as pushing a skateboard or pulling a wagon, or it can be something more complicated, like the **thrust** from a jet engine. Forces are all around us, but they are invisible—you can only see their effect.

ESSENTIAL QUESTION

What are the different forces that control movement, and what would life be like without these forces?

When you apply a force to something, what happens? If the force is big enough, you can get things moving. If you push or pull something, does it keep going? Or does it eventually stop?

WORDS TO KNOW

thrust: a force that pushes an object forward.

physicist: a scientist who studies physical forces, including matter, energy, and motion, and how these forces interact with each other.

mechanics: the working parts of something.

BCE: put after a date, BCE stands for Before Common Era and counts down to zero. CE stands for Common Era and counts up from zero. These non-religious terms correspond to BC and AD. This book was printed in 2018 CE.

natural state: according to Aristotle, the way an object behaves when nothing is acting on it.

astronomy: the study of the sun, moon, stars, planets, and space.

MECHANICS: STUDYING MOTION

Ancient scientists and philosophers from every culture were fascinated by how and why things move. These first **physicists** looked closely at the world around them and tried to explain what they saw. The study of motion and forces is called **mechanics**.

Aristotle (384–322 **BCE**) was a Greek philosopher and scientist who studied lots of things, including physics, math, and biology. By looking closely at how things moved in the world around him, he developed a theory of motion to describe what he saw.

Aristotle believed that everything had a "**natural state**" it wanted to be in. According to Aristotle, water flowed because its natural state was to move, and a stone was motionless because its natural state was to be at rest. Aristotle believed that to change something's natural state, a force must be applied to it, and the force must continue to be applied to keep it moving. Without an applied force, the object would return to its natural state.

Feel the Force!

Although there's no "Force" like the kind you see in science fiction, forces are everywhere. What forces are acting on you right now? How many can you think of?

 PS Check out this video—it might surprise you!

🔎 Veritasium forces acting

The Motion of the Heavens

One of the first ways ancient peoples studied motion was by observing the sky. By carefully watching and recording the movements of the sun, moon, planets, and stars, many different cultures used **astronomy** to create calendars. These calendars helped the Maya of Central America determine when to plant crops and told the Egyptians when the Nile River was likely to flood. What did these early calendars look like? Are they still used today?

For example, a horse cart's natural state is at rest. For it to move, a horse needs to continuously apply a force. If the horse stops, the cart will return to its natural state and stop moving. To throw a stone, you apply a force to the stone to get it moving. But, according to Aristotle, once you let go you're no longer applying a force, and the stone will fall to the ground and return to its natural state.

Aristotle's idea of a natural state makes a lot of sense, because it describes what we see around us.

Whether you roll a ball across a floor or push a book across a table, both objects will eventually come to a stop. And any projectile, whether it's a home run ball or a bullet fired from a gun, eventually comes to rest.

A bust of Aristotle made from marble, a Roman copy of a Greek bronze original by Lysippos from 330 BCE
credit: Ludovisi Collection

WORDS TO KNOW

calculus: a branch of mathematics involving calculations.

gravity: the force that pulls objects toward each other and holds you on Earth.

friction: a force that resists motion.

For almost 2,000 years Aristotle's ideas were used to explain how and why things moved. It wasn't until Isaac Newton (1643–1727) challenged these long-held beliefs about motion that the world discovered that Aristotle was only partly right.

Sir Isaac Newton was an English scientist who is famous for discovering many things, including where color comes from and an important kind of mathematics called **calculus**. But it's his study of motion and **gravity** that might be the most important.

NEWTON'S FIRST LAW OF MOTION

Since Aristotle, people had believed that all objects have their own natural states. But Newton looked at motion differently. He believed that if an object was moving, it would keep moving until something happened to stop it. And if an object wasn't moving, it wouldn't move until something got it moving. This became his first law of motion.

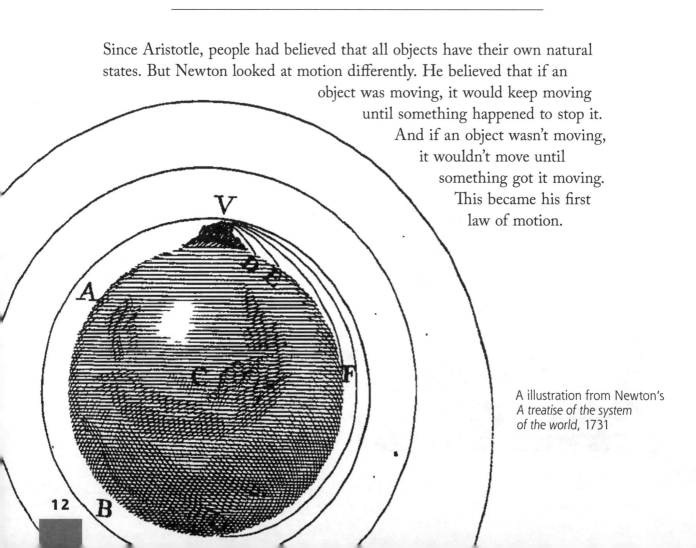

A illustration from Newton's *A treatise of the system of the world*, 1731

12

NEWTON'S FIRST LAW OF MOTION:
An object at rest will stay at rest, and an object in motion will stay in motion at the same speed and direction unless acted upon by another force.

Newton's idea might seem strange at first. How could something in motion just keep moving in the same direction, forever? If you stop peddling, your bicycle eventually slows to a stop. If you shove a book across a table, it probably won't even make it to the edge. And even the hardest hit home run ball comes down somewhere.

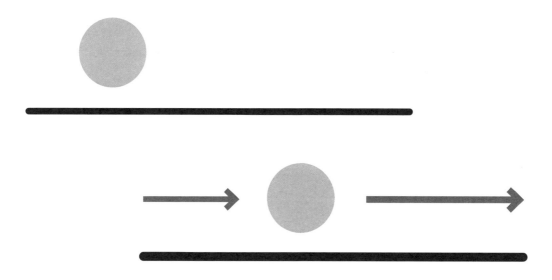

But Newton believed that without a force acting on them, bicycles, books, and baseballs would keep doing what they're doing, forever. According to Newton, a force must be at work to slow an object down and eventually stop it from moving. For most things, the force that acts on objects to slow them down is **friction**.

Friction happens when two things move against each other. There is friction between a bicycle tire and the road, and there is friction between a book and the tabletop it slides across.

WORDS TO KNOW

inertia: the resistance of an object to a change in its motion.

mass: a measure of the amount of matter in an object.

accelerate: to increase the speed of an object's movement.

velocity: a measure of an object's speed and direction.

decelerate: to decrease the speed of an object's movement.

Another way to describe Newton's first law is to say that objects resist changes in motion.

Have you noticed that when a car comes to a sudden stop, you're thrown forward against your seatbelt? And when the car lurches ahead, you're thrown back into your seat? This resistance to a change in motion has a special term: **inertia**. Your body has inertia and wants to keep doing what it's doing until another force is applied to change your motion.

The amount of inertia something has depends on its **mass**. Mass is the amount of stuff that makes up an object. Everything from ice cream to elephants has mass. The more mass an object has, the greater the amount of inertia.

Inertia is also the reason you wouldn't want to kick a bowling ball like you would kick a soccer ball. A bowling ball has much more mass than a soccer ball and needs a much larger force to get it moving. And kicking it would be very painful! Ouch!

DID YOU KNOW?

Newton's first law of motion is also called the law of inertia.

Sticking to the Ground

Have you ever been ice skating? The amount of friction between the skates and the ice is very low, letting you glide across the ice. Friction is also how your sneakers grip the pavement when you run. Without it, you wouldn't get very far! If there was no friction, an object in motion would keep moving forever—unless something else came along to stop it.

Whenever something speeds up or slows down, it's **accelerating**. Acceleration is a change in **velocity**. When you throw a ball, you're accelerating it. When you catch a ball, you're **decelerating** it. Acceleration can happen in any direction—forward or backward, up or down, even side to side. What determines how an object accelerates? Newton also tackled that problem, and figured it out with his second law of motion.

Velocity

Velocity is a measure of an object's speed and direction. When a pitcher hurls a fastball, the ball's speed is measured at 100 miles per hour. But the fastball's velocity is 100 miles per hour toward home plate. Velocity is very important in ballistics—we want to know where projectiles are headed and how soon they're going to get there!

What forces can you spot working in this photograph?

15

NEWTON'S SECOND LAW OF MOTION

NEWTON'S SECOND LAW OF MOTION:
The acceleration of an object is proportional to and in the same direction as the force applied, and inversely proportional to the mass of the object.

That's a mouthful. The second law of motion says that how something accelerates depends on just two things—the mass of the object and the force applied to it. How does the second law work, and what does it really mean?

NEWTON'S SECOND LAW SAYS THE MORE MASS AN OBJECT HAS, THE HARDER IT IS TO ACCELERATE.

RIGHT! WE HAVE TO APPLY MORE FORCE TO MOVE THE CART NOW BECAUSE WE ADDED MORE MASS.

SO DOESN'T NEWTON'S FIRST LAW MEAN THAT IT WILL TAKE MORE FORCE TO STOP THE CART, TOO?

YES, I GUESS IT DOES...

UH OH!

LOOK OUT, DEV!

AHHH!!

The more force you apply, the more you can accelerate an object. But the more massive something is, the harder it is to accelerate and the greater force you'll need to get it moving. The more things you put in the shopping cart, the more force you need to accelerate it. While it might not take much effort to push a skateboard, what would happen if you applied the same amount of force to a car? You wouldn't be able to accelerate it like you can a skateboard!

WORDS TO KNOW

proportional: corresponding in size.

inversely: when something increases in relation to a decrease in another thing or vice versa.

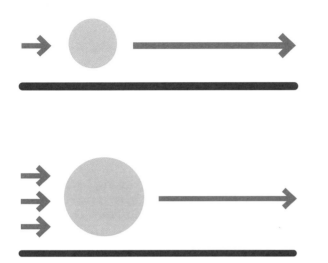

When you throw or kick a ball, why does the ball, and not your arm or leg, go flying? Forces occur when things interact with each other. When you try to shoot a goal in soccer, your foot interacts with the ball. When an arrow hits a bulls-eye, the arrow interacts with the target. How do these pairs work together to get things moving or bring them to a halt? Newton solved the problem with his third law of motion.

Forces are an important part of archery competitions.

WORDS TO KNOW

action force: the force created by one object that acts upon another.

reaction force: the force acting in the opposite direction to the action force.

recoil: to spring back suddenly as the result of an action force.

contact force: a force that occurs when two objects are touching each other.

NEWTON'S THIRD LAW OF MOTION

NEWTON'S THIRD LAW OF MOTION: For every action (force), there is an equal and opposite reaction (force).

Forces always come in pairs. When your foot applies a force to a ball, the ball applies an equal force in the opposite direction to your foot! Your foot striking the ball is the **action force** and the ball pushing back against your foot is the **reaction force**.

If the forces are equal, how does one object move more, or accelerate more, than another? Why does a kicked ball sail into the sky instead of sending your foot backwards?

Remember, acceleration depends on force and mass. If the forces are equal, then the object with the least mass will accelerate the most. When you kick a ball, the forces between your foot and the ball are equal, but the masses are not the same.

Compared to you, the soccer ball has very little mass. When you apply the force, the ball accelerates quickly in the direction you kick. The reaction force of the ball accelerates you in the opposite direction, but it barely slows your foot down, thanks to your greater mass. But remember, if you tried to kick a bowling ball—ouch!

Equal and Opposite

Equal and opposite force pairs are everywhere. When a bat hits a ball, the bat exerts an action force on the ball and the ball exerts a reaction force on the bat. But because the ball has less mass than the bat, the ball accelerates the most in the direction of the swing! The acceleration of the bat in the opposite direction is called **recoil**.

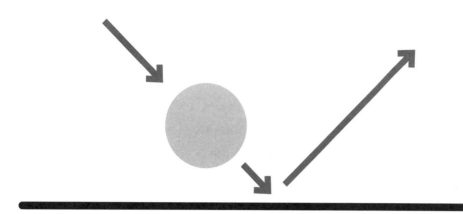

So far, you've learned that forces are needed to get things moving, and to bring them to a stop. But what's going on when things aren't moving? Are there still forces acting on a ball before it's struck or on a car parked on the street? You might already know the answer—gravity!

DID YOU KNOW?

Have you ever high-fived someone and felt it sting your hand? Did they feel it too? That's because you're both exerting forces on each other!

GREAT GRAVITY!

Gravity is everywhere. It keeps planets circling their stars and makes black holes black. Here on Earth, gravity is the reason you fall when you trip. It's also why we say, "What goes up, must come down." Everything that has mass, from the smallest atom to the farthest galaxy, feels the force of gravity.

Most forces we see in action are forces that push or pull things, such as the forces you use when steering a shopping cart through the grocery store or playing a game of tug-of-war. These are **contact forces**. Contact forces happen when things contact, or touch, each other. But gravity is different.

Gravity works at a distance, without objects having to touch each other. It pulls everything together, even the farthest galaxies. Isaac Newton discovered that gravity is universal, which means that almost everything in the universe exerts a force on everything else. And just as with other forces, we can't see gravity, but we can see it bring a baseball into a fielder's glove or feel it when we leap to take a jump shot.

The amount of gravity an object has depends on its mass. Big things, such as planets and stars, have a lot of gravity, while small things, such as people and basketballs, have much less. Because Earth is so massive, you feel its pull much more strongly than the planet feels your pull on it.

Mass and Weight

Sometimes, people confuse mass and weight. While mass is a measure of how much matter makes up an object, weight is a measure of how strongly gravity pulls on a mass. On the moon, your weight would be just one-sixth of your weight on Earth, but your mass would still be the same!

Go here to see how much you'd weigh on other planets!

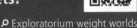

Exploratorium weight worlds

Both the planet and the astronaut are exerting a gravitational force on each other. Which force is stronger? Why?

Gravity also depends on the distance between things. The closer things are, the stronger the force of gravity is between them. But if they move apart, the pull between them weakens.

For centuries, people have been studying gravity. In the sixteenth century, Galileo Galilei (1564–1642), an Italian scientist and philosopher, discovered something very important about gravity and how it affects falling objects. In Galileo's time, people believed that heavy objects fell faster than lighter ones. Galileo wanted to test this, so he came up with an experiment.

Legend has it that Galileo climbed to the top of the Leaning Tower of Pisa in Italy and dropped two spheres of different masses. He timed how long each took to reach the ground—the two spheres hit the earth at the same time! This means that a falling object's acceleration doesn't depend on its mass. The earth's gravity accelerates everything at the same rate, whether it's a pebble or a person.

ESSENTIAL QUESTION

What are the different forces that control movement, and what would life be like without these forces?

Gravity is always there, pulling everything back toward the earth. So how do all these laws and forces affect the movement and paths of projectiles? The different forces that control motion, including gravity, all affect the way projectiles move through the air. In the next chapter, we'll look at some projectiles and how they behave!

As the World Turns

Why don't we feel the moon's gravity? Even though the moon is 238,900 miles away, the moon's gravity pulls on Earth and everything on the planet. Because we're so far from the moon and our mass is so small, we don't notice the moon's pull. But big things on Earth—including oceans—do! In fact, ocean tides come from the sun and moon tugging on the oceans as the Earth rotates.

 To learn more about how gravity causes tides, check out this video!

🔎 Crash Course tides

OBSERVING FORCES OF MOTION

When something moves, a lot is going on that we don't see. But we can make deductions based on our observations of different movements! Try moving different objects on different surfaces and see what you learn.

➤ **Find a large, flat surface, such as a floor or tabletop.** Make sure the surface can't be damaged by water or by rolling or sliding objects! Try rolling a round object, such as a ball, and watch its motion carefully. How far does it go? Does something stop it, or does it stop on its own?

➤ **Next, try sliding a book or other flat object.** How does its motion compare to a rolled object? Does something stop it, or does it seem to stop on its own?

➤ **Now, try sliding or rolling a plastic container.** First, get it moving while it's empty. How does its motion compare to the first two objects? Now, put water into the container (be sure to put the cap on or seal it) and get it moving. How does the full container's motion compare to the empty container?

Questions to think about

* What stops the object's motion? Is it the same for each item?

* Which object stops the quickest? Why?

* Which object goes the farthest and why?

* Why do you think the motions of the objects are different?

* Does the type of motion (rolling or sliding) make a difference?

* Does the weight of an object affect its motion?

* Which object takes the most force to move? Which takes the least? Why?

Try This!

Try exploring the movements of other objects. What happens when you throw a ball? What gets it moving and what stops it? Do bikes or skateboards roll forever?

WORDS TO KNOW

deduction: a conclusion reached by reasoning or evidence.

TRICKY INERTIA

Newton's first law and the idea of inertia can help explain how and why things move, and why some things are harder than others to get going—and to stop. Can Isaac Newton help you get a coin into a cup without touching the coin?

▶ Place a playing card or an index card on top of a glass or clear plastic cup. Place a coin on top of the card.

▶ Can you think of a way to get the coin into the cup without touching the cup? First, try pulling the card slowly. What happens to the coin? What else can you try?

▶ Try flicking or hitting the index card. What happens to the coin?

Questions to think about

✱ Can you flick the card fast enough so the coin simply drops into the cup?

✱ Can you describe what's happening using Newton's first law and inertia?

✱ What happens when you move the card more slowly? Why does the speed of the card matter?

✱ What force makes the coin fall into the cup?

Magic!

A classic magician's trick is to pull a tablecloth out from under the dishes on a table, leaving them on the table! Try this at home with plastic or paper plates and cups. How is this like the coin and cup? What law of motion does a magician use in this trick?

Try This!

When the card is removed quickly, the coin resists moving with the card because its inertia is greater than the force applied by the card. With the card out of the way, the coin falls into the cup. Challenge someone to see if they can figure out how to get the coin in the cup. Resist giving them hints!

NEWTON'S SECOND LAW OF MOTION

Newton's second law says that the acceleration of an object depends on the object's mass and the force applied to it. Can we see the second law in action?

▶ **Find a flat, open area to move a wagon or other small cart on wheels.** Push or pull the empty cart several times in different directions. Get a feel for how the cart moves when it is empty.

▶ **Place an object or two in the cart.** Try moving the cart again. Is there a difference?

▶ **Keep loading the cart up with more objects!** How does this change the movement?

Questions to think about

* When do you apply the most force and the least force?

* Is it easier to accelerate the cart when it is empty or full?

* When you push the cart, how does it move?

* Is the cart harder to stop when it's full or when it's empty?

* Can you use Newton's laws to describe the difference?

Try This!

If your cart didn't have wheels, would it be easier or harder to push? Find a container without wheels and repeat your experiment. What are your observations?

NEWTON'S
THIRD LAW OF MOTION

Newton's third law says that for every action, there is an equal and opposite reaction. Test this yourself!

❯ **Inflate a balloon.** Once you've blown up the balloon, pinch the open end closed with a binder clip or clothespin. Don't tie the balloon closed!

❯ **Attach your balloon to a small toy car.** Make sure the opening of the balloon is pointing in the opposite direction you want your car to move. Use tape to hold the balloon firmly in place on the car.

❯ **Aim the car in the direction you want it to travel.** Make sure its path is clear! You don't want anything to interfere with the car's motion.

❯ **Remove the clip from the balloon** and watch the car go!

Questions to think about

✱ What's happening when you remove the clip?

✱ What direction does the air travel compared to the motion of the car?

✱ What direction does the car move compared to the escaping air?

✱ How does this demonstrate Newton's third law?

Try This!

How does changing the amount of air in the balloon affect the car's acceleration? Try using balloons of different sizes and shapes. How do they affect the motion of the car? How does the surface the car is on affect its speed and distance moved?

PISA PARTY

In the late sixteenth century, Galileo Galilei climbed to the top of the Leaning Tower of Pisa to conduct an experiment to find out if heavy objects fall faster than lighter ones. What do you think? Will a heavier object fall faster than a lighter one? Choose two balls of the same size but different masses to experiment with.

❯ **Find a safe height for your ball drop.** Make sure the objects you're dropping can't damage what they land on, or anything else!

❯ **If you use a video camera to record the experiment,** be sure it's set up far enough away that it can't be damaged.

❯ **In your engineering notebook, number each test so you can record what happens.** What do you think will happen when you drop the two balls at the same time? What is your hypothesis?

❯ **From a safe height, carefully drop the two balls** at the same time.

❯ **Repeat your experiment several times!** It's important that you repeat your experiment so your results are consistent.

DID YOU KNOW?

Although nobody is really sure if Galileo performed his experiment from the Leaning Tower of Pisa, the tower really does lean!

Follow this link to learn about the tower and why it's tipped, but hasn't fallen over!

🔍 why Pisa tower does not fall

> ❯ **Carefully observe how the balls fall.** If you have a video camera that records in slow motion, use it!

> ❯ **Record the results of each test in your engineering notebook.** Does one hit before the other, or do they land at the same time?

Questions to think about

* ✱ How did the balls drop?

* ✱ Did one hit before the other?

* ✱ Did they hit at the same time?

Watch Out Below!

The air applies friction to falling objects, which can affect the outcome of this famous experiment. What happens when you take the air away? While we can't all travel to the moon to drop bowling balls and feathers, some people do have access to an airless chamber!

 Watch what happens to falling objects in an airless chamber! 🔍 Brian Cox chamber

Try This!

Repeat your experiment and use balls or objects of the same mass, but different size. Do the results change? Why or why not? What about objects of the same mass, but different shapes?

Galileo's experiment showed that the force of gravity accelerates everything downward at the same rate. It doesn't matter how much mass an object has. A bowling ball and a basketball dropped at the same time from the same height will hit the ground together. This means that whether you kick a ball, fire an arrow, or launch a rocket, gravity treats them all the same way.

Chapter 2

PROJECTILE MOTION:
TRACKING TRAJECTORIES

What's the difference between a ground ball and a fly ball? Between the motion of a basketball during a free throw and a ball being dribbled? Or the path of a skateboard down the street and the path of one on a ramp? They all have different **trajectories**.

A trajectory is the path an object takes as it moves. A rolling ball has a straight trajectory because it moves in one direction. A dribbled basketball also has a straight trajectory because it moves only up and down. A ground ball is an example of **horizontal** motion. Horizontal motion can be left or right, forward or backward—any motion that isn't up or down. A dribbled basketball has **vertical** motion, which is motion that is only up or down.

ESSENTIAL QUESTION

When might it be useful to know the height and distance a projectile has traveled?

trajectory: the curve a body travels along in its path through space.

horizontal: straight across from side to side.

vertical: straight up and down.

ballistic trajectory: the trajectory of an object acted upon by only gravity and air resistance.

Projectiles don't follow straight trajectories. They fly over fields and fall into gloves or beyond outfield walls. They sail through the air, hitting the bulls-eye on a target 100 feet away. Projectiles have both horizontal and vertical motion because they are most often launched at angles. Together, they determine whether a ball is a home run or an out, or if an arrow hits the bulls-eye or misses the target.

DID YOU KNOW?

Can you think of objects that move only vertically? What about things that move only horizontally?

BALLISTIC MOTION

When it comes to ballistics and the motion of projectiles, gravity is (almost) everything. When you throw a ball into the air, you apply a force to the ball to send it on its way. But once the ball leaves your hand, you're no longer applying a force. According to Newton's first law, the ball should keep moving in a straight line at the same speed. But does it?

As soon as the ball leaves your hand, the only force acting on it is gravity. This is the same for bullets, baseballs, arrows, and bombs. When the only force acting on a projectile is gravity, it has ballistic motion. Gravity is always pulling projectiles downward, curving their paths into a **ballistic trajectory**.

What force will act on this baseball once it leaves the pitcher's hand?

PROJECTILE SCIENCE

WORDS TO KNOW

parabola: an upside down, U-shaped curve that is a cross section of a cone.

rate: the speed of something measured in an amount of time, such as miles per hour or feet per second.

lofted: an object that is propelled up.

The shape of a ballistic trajectory is called a **parabola**. Parabolas can be tall, such as the path of a punted football, or they can be almost flat, such as the path of a bullet.

Parabolas are the result of two kinds of motion: horizontal motion and vertical motion.

When studying ballistics, it's helpful to look at horizontal and vertical motion separately to understand how they affect the motion of projectiles.

Powerful Parabolas

Have you seen a parabola? Parabolas aren't just found in the motions of projectiles. The mirrors inside car headlights are shaped like parabolas, helping to illuminate roads at night. Parabolas are also used in bridges to make them lighter and stronger. Where else do you see this mighty shape? Want to see a parabola in action? Water follows a parabolic path, too! If you have a squirt gun or a hose, you can watch the water fall to the ground on a ballistic trajectory!

HORIZONTAL MOTION

You've seen horizontal motion in action. When a ball rolls across a room or when you slide in your socks on a slippery floor, that's horizontal motion. Forward, backward, or side-to-side, horizontal motion is everywhere. Because it's easy to move horizontally, it's easy to calculate the **rate**, or speed, of an object when it's moving!

Horizontal motion shows us how Newton's first law of motion works. When a ball is moving, it will keep moving at the same speed and in the same direction until another force comes along to change its velocity.

Unless the ball runs into a wall or your shoe, friction will be the force that slows and stops the ball.

But what about a **lofted** soccer ball or an arrow? A projectile has horizontal motion, but without friction between itself and the ground, it should continue with the same horizontal speed and direction forever, according to the first law. But that doesn't happen!

Friction Facts

There are two basic types of friction. Static friction occurs when something rests on a surface, such as your shoes on the pavement or a car parked on the street. Kinetic friction happens between objects that are moving against each other. A sled sliding across snow or a ball rolling along the ground are examples of kinetic friction.

A projectile's horizontal velocity does stay the same until something stops it, such as a fielder's glove or a wall. It's the vertical motion of the projectile that brings an arrow's flight to an end and brings even the hardest hit ball back to Earth. What goes up, must come down—thanks to the vertical motion caused by gravity.

DID YOU KNOW?

Basketball players often have their vertical leap measured. It tells them how high they can jump! What is your vertical leap?

VERTICAL MOTION

When you dribble a basketball or ride an elevator, you are experiencing vertical motion. Newton's first law should work for something that's moving horizontally or vertically. But you don't need to apply a force to make your tablet or a book fall. You just need to drop it.

When you drop something, Newton's first law says that it should stay right where it is. After all, you're not pushing it up or down, so you're not applying a force, right?

But that's not what happens. As soon as you let go, an object falls until something stops it—usually the ground. That's because the force of gravity accelerates anything you drop as soon as you let go.

In fact, just by holding it, you are applying a force to keep the object from falling. This force is called the **normal force**. When you sit in a chair, gravity tries to make you fall by accelerating you downward. But the chair stops that from happening.

Gravity is the action force, and the chair applies the normal force, which is the reaction force!

Thanks to Galileo's experiment, we know that gravity accelerates everything equally. It doesn't matter how much mass an object has—a piano falls at the same rate as a pickle. But knowing just how much gravity accelerates something can help us understand projectile motion!

No matter how an object is moving, the force of gravity is always causing an acceleration toward the center of the earth, even if you throw a ball straight up. If you toss a ball straight up, gravity decelerates the ball, slowing its speed until it starts to fall back to the earth.

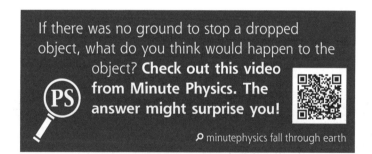

If there was no ground to stop a dropped object, what do you think would happen to the object? **Check out this video from Minute Physics. The answer might surprise you!**

🔍 minutephysics fall through earth

But objects such as basketballs and rockets don't move only up and down. If they did, they'd be much less interesting! A baseball hit to the outfield can be a home run only if it travels far and high enough to fly over the fence.

To become a home run, a well-struck baseball needs to combine vertical and horizontal motion. To do that, the ball must be hit at an **angle.**

When a projectile is launched at an angle, it has vertical motion and horizontal motion. An arrow has horizontal motion toward its target, and gravity accelerates its vertical motion.

So, are vertical and horizontal motion independent of each other, or does one affect the other?

THE DROP TEST

Imagine a coin shot horizontally from a slingshot. At the same time, a coin is dropped from the same height as the slingshot without any horizontal motion. Does Galileo's experiment still work? Are vertical and horizontal velocity independent or does one kind of motion affect the other?

A Delta II rocket launches at an angle and arcs across the night sky. Can you spot the parabola? What kinds of motions are displayed here?
credit: NASA/Bill Ingalls

You might think that the coin with horizontal motion would take longer to hit the ground, because it has a greater distance to travel.

But both coins still hit the ground at the same time! That's because horizontal and vertical motion really are independent, or separate, from each other.

Even a bullet fired from a gun would hit the ground at the same time as a bullet dropped from the same height! And when a projectile is fired at an angle, its horizontal velocity stays the same during its flight, but its vertical velocity is always changing.

Gravity doesn't care if a projectile has horizontal motion or not, it pulls on everything the same way. Knowing that the horizontal and vertical motions of projectiles are independent is very helpful, because it lets us figure out some interesting things about a projectile's ballistic motion.

HOW HIGH CAN YOU THROW?

Imagine a long fly ball hit into the outfield. At the beginning of its flight, the ball is rising into the air. But gravity is pulling on it, slowing its vertical motion until, for a brief instant, the ball isn't rising or falling. This is the projectile's **maximum height**! From there, gravity continues to accelerate the ball downward until it hits the ground or lands in a fielder's glove.

How high did the ball go? Since we know the acceleration of gravity, we can use this information and the time it takes the ball to fall from the top of its parabola to find out its maximum height.

WORDS TO KNOW

variable: a symbol that holds the place for information that may change.

range: the distance a projectile travels horizontally.

We can use a little math to figure it out with an equation: $h = \frac{1}{2}g \times t^2$

- **h** = height of the ball, in feet

- **g** = acceleration due to gravity, which is 32.2 feet per second, per second

- **t** = time the ball takes to fall from its maximum height to the ground, in seconds

This math might seem difficult, but you can do it! Let's say that the ball is in the air for 6 seconds. That means it took 3 seconds to go up and 3 seconds to come back down. How high did the ball go?

- First, multiply the times **t**, by itself:
  3 × 3 = 9

- Next, multiply your result by **g** (which is 32.2):
  9 × 32.2 = 289.8

- Finally, divide your result by two to get **h**, the height of the ball:
  289.8 ÷ 2 = 144.9

If a ball is in the air for 6 seconds, then it reached a height of about 145 feet! You can figure this for any projectile. All you need to know is how long it stayed in the air! That's because Earth's gravity always accelerates things at the same rate!

By learning how to do the kind of equations that relate to how projectiles fly, you can figure out lots of different things, which is useful when you enter an archery contest or join a basketball team. While you might not pause the game to figure out the trajectory of the basketball, if you've already done your homework, you've got a better shot at making the shot!

DID YOU KNOW?
When you see a letter such as *h* or *g* in an equation, don't panic! These are called **variables**. They're used to hold the places of things we don't know, or things we're going find out!

HOW FAR?

Now that you can find the height of a projectile, can you find out how far it goes? The distance a projectile travels horizontally is called its **range**.

How do people determine the distance of a home run? They don't use a measuring tape! Instead, they use mathematics. **You can read about it here!**

🔍 MLB HR-DIS

Finding a projectile's range can be easy—you simply measure it if you have a long enough tape measure. But you also use math to find out how far a baseball or an arrow has traveled if you know two things: how long the projectile is in the air and its horizontal velocity.

Here is an equation we can use to help find the range of a projectile if we know the horizontal speed and its flight time: $d = r \times t$

- d = horizontal distance, or range, in feet

- r = rate or horizontal velocity, in feet per second

- t = flight time, in seconds

Suppose you kick a soccer ball at an angle, sending it down the field with a horizontal velocity of 10 feet per second. Using a stopwatch, you determine that it was in the air for a total of 8 seconds. How far did it go?

Multiply the horizontal velocity (r) by the flight time (t) to get the distance (d).

$$10 \times 8 = 80$$

The ball traveled 80 feet!

Flying Long

The longest home run ever recorded was by Joey Meyer (1962–) of the Denver Zephyrs. His home run was 582 feet. The longest goal in soccer was scored by goalie Asmir Begović (1987–), who scored from 100.5 yards. What other records would you like to know?

WORDS TO KNOW

maximum range: the greatest distance a projectile travels horizontally.

parallel: two lines always the same distance apart.

perpendicular: a line at an angle of 90 degrees to another line or surface. The two lines form a corner, called a right angle.

Why does this work? Because a projectile's horizontal velocity will stay the same unless a force acts to change it—for example, a ball hitting the ground or an arrow striking a target.

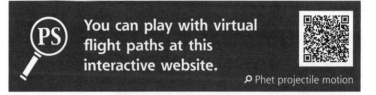

(PS) You can play with virtual flight paths at this interactive website.

🔎 Phet projectile motion

LAUNCH ANGLE

You can calculate the height and range of a projectile using some simple math. But how would you find out the best way to fire a projectile so it travels the greatest distance? This is called **maximum range**.

A projectile is usually fired at an angle between 0 and 90 degrees, or horizontal and vertical. Horizontal is 0 degrees, or **parallel** to the ground, and vertical is 90 degrees, or **perpendicular** to the ground.

Math Practice!

You can calculate the range of a projectile if you know its time in flight and horizontal velocity. Try a few of the problems below. You can draw pictures, create diagrams, make lists—whichever method works best for you! Find the answers on page 118.

› A football is kicked with a horizontal velocity of 22 feet per second and has a flight time of 2 seconds. How far did the football travel?

› A catapult flings a heavy boulder. It takes 5 seconds to reach its target with a horizontal velocity of 20 feet per second. How far away was the target?

› An arrow travels 200 feet. If its horizontal velocity was 50 feet per second, how long did it take to reach its target?

Imagine you're leading a band of archers against a enemy, and you want to be as far from them as possible when you unleash your attack. Firing straight up isn't a good idea—the arrows will probably come right back down on the archers themselves. Firing straight ahead won't work, either. Gravity will pull the arrows to the ground long before they reach the enemy.

To get the greatest range, a projectile should be launched halfway between vertical and horizontal, which is 45 degrees. This way, half of the force acting on the projectile goes toward vertical motion and half goes to horizontal motion. As long as the amount of force between them is the same, you'll get the greatest range out of your projectiles!

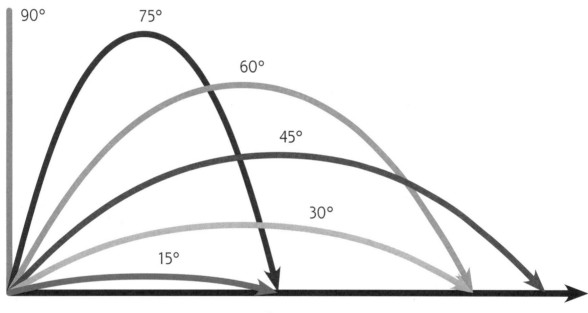

Distance

Now that you have a good grasp of the different forces affecting projectiles, let's look at some of the tools and techniques people have used to send things flying farther and faster!

ESSENTIAL QUESTION

When might it be useful to know the height and distance a projectile has traveled?

FIND THE HORIZONTAL VELOCITY

You can calculate the horizontal velocity of an object if you know how long it takes to go a certain distance. Try it out! You'll use a tube propped up at an angle to experiment with a rolling ball.

❯ At one end of a flat table, tape a cardboard tube, such as an empty paper towel roll, to the edge of a stack of books or a small box about 5 or 6 inches high. Tape the other end of the tube to the table. Make sure the tube is as straight as possible.

❯ Measure and place a piece of tape 2 feet from the bottom of the tube. Make sure it's in the path of a ball rolled through the tube.

❯ Gently place a marble or ball in the tube. Don't push it! Let it roll!

If you're a big baseball fan, you might hear people talking about a batter's launch angle! **Check out this article about one player's attempt to hit the ball further by changing the angle he swings his bat!**

PS

🔍 Wil Myers launch angle

❯ Start the timer when the marble hits the table. Stop the timer when the marble crosses the piece of tape. Record your observations in your engineering notebook.

❯ Do this several times. For each trial, calculate the speed of the ball in feet per second, using the formula for rate (speed):

$$r = d \div t$$

Activity

▶ **Divide the distance (d) by the time (t) to obtain the rate of speed (r).**

▶ **Now, calculate the average speed for all the trials.** Start by adding up all different rates.

▶ **Divide that total** by the number of trials.

▶ **Record your result!** This is the average speed of your marble.

Questions to think about

★ How close are the speeds in each trial?

★ What things might change the speed of the marble in your experiment?

★ Why do you think using the tube is better than rolling the marble by hand?

★ What forces are acting on the marble when it's in the tube? When it leaves the tube?

★ If you had a large enough table, how far do you think the marble would roll?

★ Would a carpet or rug instead of a table change the results of the experiment?

Try This!

Try the experiment again, but this time use a marble or ball of a different mass. Does the mass of the ball affect its speed? Why or why not? Change the steepness of the tube. Does it affect the speed of the ball? Why or why not?

GREAT GRAVITY!

When something falls, the force of gravity is pulling it toward the center of the earth. But how much does gravity accelerate an object when you drop it? Find out by doing some math!

▶ **Choose a height for your drop.** This should be at least 3 feet high. Measure carefully! You'll need to drop objects from the same height each time. Record the height of the drop in your engineering notebook.

▶ **From the height you picked, drop your object.** Carefully time—in seconds—how long it takes the object to hit the ground from your measured height.

▶ **Drop the same object at least five times** and record how long it takes to hit the ground. Calculate the average drop time in seconds.

▶ **Using the same drop height, try two more objects of different masses.** Be sure to record at least five drops for each!

▶ **Calculate the acceleration of gravity following these instructions and record your answer in your engineering notebook!**

DID YOU KNOW?

Since everything that falls on Earth accelerates at the same rate (32.2 feet per second, per second), physicists use the lowercase "g" to represent the acceleration of gravity. It just makes it easier to work with instead of writing "32.2 feet per second, per second" all the time!

$$a = 2d \div t^2$$

d = the drop distance (in feet)

t = the average drop time (in seconds)

a = the acceleration due to gravity

* Suppose d is 6 feet and t is 4 seconds. Multiply the height of your drop by 2: d x 2. For example, 6 x 2 = 12

* Second, multiply the average drop time by itself: t x t. For example, 4 x 4 = 16

* Finally, calculate a (acceleration) by dividing the results of the first step by the second step: a = (d x 2) ÷ (t x t). For example, 12 ÷16 = 0.75

❯ **Repeat your calculations for the other objects.**

❯ **Next, calculate the average acceleration (a).** First, add all the values you calculated. Then, divide that sum by the number of experiments you performed. This is how you calculate the acceleration of gravity!

Consider This!

Gravity accelerates everything at a rate of 32.2 feet per second, per second. That means after one second, a dropped book will have a speed of 32.2 feet per second. But because it's accelerating, the book's speed is also increasing every second—by 32.2 feet per second! So, after two seconds, it's moving at a speed of 64.4 seconds, and after three seconds, it's moving at 96.6 feet per second. That's about 65 miles per hour!

Questions to think about

* Why is it important to do the experiment several times?

* Why is using the average important?

* Does the acceleration depend on the mass of the object?

* What would Galileo have to say about this?

* Do you think the results would change if you tried the experiment at a friend's house? In a different country? On a different planet?

Try This!

Try a different height. Do you get the same results for a? Why or why not? Try using a flat piece of paper, a feather, or other very light object.

GALILEO'S EXPERIMENT, TAKE TWO!

Galileo demonstrated that all objects dropped from the same height accelerate at the same rate and hit the ground at the same time. But what if one object has horizontal motion while the other does not? Will they still reach the ground at the same time?

❯ If you're using a video camera, be sure to set it up in a place where the coins can't damage it.

❯ Place a ruler at one corner of a table, parallel with one edge of the table. Leave enough space between the ruler and the edge of the table for a coin.

❯ Place one coin at the end of the ruler. Slide the end with the coin off the table, but don't let the ruler tip!

❯ At the other end of the ruler, place another coin on the table. The coin should be between the ruler and the edge of the table, against the ruler and the table's edge.

❯ Strike the end of the ruler with the coin that sits on the table. Hit the ruler toward the table's edge, so that it pushes the coin off the table. You might have to hit the ruler with some force!

❯ Listen carefully to the sound of the two coins hitting the floor!

❯ Repeat this several times. Record what you see and hear in your engineering notebook.

Questions to think about

* Which coin hits the floor first?

* What is the difference in the motion of the two coins?

* What would happen if the coin that has horizontal motion was launched at an upward angle? Would it change when it hit the ground?

Try This!

Try launching one coin at an angle. Which coin will hit the ground first? How will that affect the motion of the coin? What if one coin is dropped from a different height? Would that change the results of the experiment?

Theory of General Relativity

In 1915, the physicist Albert Einstein (1879–1955) came up with a new way to look at gravity. In his theory of general relativity, Einstein described gravity as distortion in space and time caused by an object's mass. The more massive something is, the more it can bend space and time! In fact, things with lots of mass, such as stars, can even bend the paths of light from distant stars! And the most massive objects, black holes, have such strong gravity that nothing—not even light—can escape!

 Check out this demonstration of Einstein's theory!

🔎 Brian Greene general relativity

HOW HIGH IS HIGH?

Could you use some hang time? If you know how long a projectile is in the air, you can figure out its maximum height! How high can you get?

❯ **Throw, kick, or launch a projectile!** Use something very safe, such as a tennis ball, and launch it in an outdoor space.

❯ **Try launching at several different angles and record what you see.** They don't have to be perfect! You can record "straight up" or "mostly straight up," for example.

❯ **Have a friend record how long the projectile stays in the air.** Start the timer as soon as the projectile starts moving and stop it as soon as it hits the ground. Using a countdown can help!

❯ **Record the result in your engineering notebook.** Record several attempts, and then switch places with your friend and repeat the experiment.

❯ **Calculate the height of your projectiles with this formula.**

$$h = \tfrac{1}{2}\, g \times t^2$$

h = height of the projectile, in feet

g = acceleration due to gravity,
which is 32.2 feet per second, per second

t = time the ball takes to fall from its maximum
height to the ground, in seconds

Activity

* First, divide the time you recorded by 2.
  For example, if the projectile was in the air for 4 seconds, it spent 2 seconds going up and 2 seconds coming down. You need to know how long it took to come down.

* Second, multiply the time (t) in seconds, by itself: $t \times t$.
  For example, $2 \times 2 = 4$

* Next, multiply your result by g, which is 32.2.
  For example, $4 \times 32.2 = 128.8$

* Finally, divide your result in half to get h, the height of the projectile.
  For example, $128.8 \div 2 = 64.4$ feet.

Questions to think about

* What angle gives you the most height?

* What things seem to affect the height of the projectile?

* Who got the most height, and why?

* Can you explain the winner using the laws of motion?

* Why is horizontal motion not important when figuring out the height?

Try This!

Try dropping a projectile from a height you can measure, such as the height of a basketball hoop. Find the height using the time it takes to fall. How does it match your measurements? If you knew the height an object was dropped from, could you calculate how long it took to reach the ground?

LAUNCH ANGLE TEST

What launch angle will send a projectile the greatest distance? Using a yardstick equipped with a protractor to measure angles, you can launch rubber bands to see,

❯ **On a yardstick, mark a spot at about 22 inches.**

❯ **To attach a protractor to the yardstick,** place the origin (the center dot or circle) of the protractor at the 22-inch mark. Align the protractor so that the 90-degree angle (the baseline) points along the yardstick, and that 0 degrees is perpendicular to the yardstick. Then secure the protractor to the yardstick with clear tape, being careful not to cover up the angles on the protractor.

❯ **Make a loop of string.** It should be long enough to hang 1 to 2 inches below the protractor from the origin.

❯ **Place a pushpin at the origin.** Hang the string on the pushpin.

❯ **Tape a binder clip or other small weight** to the bottom of the string.

❯ **Choose a launch angle and record it in your engineering notebook.** Hold the yardstick so that the string hangs freely across the protractor.

❯ **Prepare your projectile.** Loop a rubber band around the end of the yardstick farthest from the protractor.

❯ **Fire your rubber band!** Each time you launch a rubber band, be sure to stretch it the same amount. Place a mark on the yardstick to help you remember how far you stretched!

❯ **Record several different launch angles!** Make sure that you're launching from the same height off the ground each time.

Activity

Questions to think about

* Which launch angle gives your rubber band the greatest range?

* Why is it important to keep the height of the launcher the same?

* Why does the rubber band need to be stretched the same length each time?

* What forces affect the rubber band when it's in flight?

Try This!

Try stretching the rubber band a different amount. How does this affect the distance? What happens if you launch your rubber band projectile at 0 degrees or 90 degrees? Can you create a way to launch something other than a rubber band?

Chapter 3

SLINGSHOTS, CATAPULTS, AND CANNONS:
MECHANICAL ENERGY

What's the fastest you can throw a baseball? How far can you kick a football? With years of practice and training, the best athletes in the world can kick, hurl, and toss objects incredible speeds and distances.

But even the fastest and the strongest athletes can't throw a boulder the length of a soccer field or fire a pitch at 300 miles per hour. To hurl projectiles farther and faster, people need the help of **machines**.

ESSENTIAL QUESTION

Why do people keep inventing new and improved ways of sending projectiles through the air?

MACHINES

What do hammers, wheels, and bows have in common? All are examples of machines. Machines can be complicated, such as an airplane, or they can be simple, such as a hammer. Machines can come in different sizes and can have many uses.

A machine is anything that helps you do **work**. In this book, when we talk about work, we're not talking about your homework or a person's job. Work is done when a force moves an object. And machines can make this work easier. A system of **pulleys** does work by helping lift heavy things you could never lift on your own, while a bow can shoot an arrow farther and faster than even the best Olympic athlete could ever throw.

DID YOU KNOW?

Which sports make use of machines to get things moving farther and faster? What would baseball be like without a bat? What about ping-pong without a paddle? Lots of sports use machines to get things moving. Can you think of some others?

One of the earliest examples of a machine is the **atlatl**. This spear-thrower helps increase the distance and speed a person can throw a spear.

Atlatls help people throw spears farther and faster by acting as an extension of the thrower's arm. The atlatl's extra length and mass increase the amount of work a thrower can do by giving the spear more **energy**. To get bigger projectiles moving farther and faster, you'll need all the energy you can find!

WORDS TO KNOW

kinetic energy: energy associated with motion.

potential energy: energy that is stored.

gravitational potential energy: the energy an object possesses because of its position in a gravitational field.

mechanical energy: energy that uses physical parts you can see, such as the parts of a machine. It is related to motion and height.

ENERGY

You probably hear the word "energy" a lot. There's solar energy from the sun, chemical energy in batteries, electrical energy, and nuclear energy, just to name a few.

Do you have a lot of energy? Sure! When you're running a race or riding a bicycle, you have **kinetic energy**. Kinetic energy is the energy of motion. A basketball sailing toward the hoop and a car cruising down the road both have kinetic energy. When you apply a force to something and it moves, you're increasing its kinetic energy. The amount of kinetic energy something has depends on its mass and velocity. A moving car has more kinetic energy than a bicycle going the same speed, and a hard-struck soccer ball has more kinetic energy than a soft pass.

But things don't have to be moving to have energy. When you pick up a ball, you're giving it kinetic energy. But if you stop lifting and just hold the ball, where did its energy go? The kinetic energy is changed into something called **potential energy**. You can think of potential energy as stored energy, kind of like a battery.

Runners at a starting line have potential energy. When they take off, their potential energy is changed into kinetic energy.

If you drop the ball, the force of gravity accelerates it, turning the potential energy back into kinetic energy. This potential energy is called **gravitational potential energy**.

Gravitational potential energy depends on an object's mass and height. The higher something is, the more potential energy it has. A book on a bookshelf has more gravitational potential energy than a book on the floor. And a big dictionary has more potential energy than the small paperback on the shelf because the dictionary has more mass!

There are many kinds of potential energy. Batteries hold electric potential energy. Food has chemical potential energy, which our bodies change into kinetic energy to get us moving. Springs, rubber bands, and even twisted string have elastic potential energy, which becomes kinetic energy when these are released.

Together, kinetic and potential energy make **mechanical energy**. The ability to do work, or to get moving, is called mechanical energy. While you can't see kinetic and potential energy, you can see the work that they do.

Imagine a marble balanced at the top of a ramp. What kind of energy does it have? If the marble starts to roll down the ramp, what kind of energy does it have now? Imagine there's a cup at the bottom of the ramp. When the marble hits it, the cup goes flying! What is that energy called?

DID YOU KNOW?

Have you heard the phrase "the bigger they are, the harder they fall"? How does it relate to potential energy?

Conservation of Energy

Where does energy go? When a ball rolls to a stop, where did its energy go? Energy doesn't disappear—it can only be turned into another kind of energy. Friction can transform the energy of motion into heat, while placing a book on a shelf transforms its kinetic energy into potential energy. This is called the conservation of energy. It means that energy can't be created or destroyed—it can only be changed from one form to another. In fact, all the energy in the universe changes only from one kind of energy to another.

The kinetic and potential energy of an object can change from one form to the other, depending on how the object is moving and its position. When the marble is at the top of the ramp, it has only potential energy. But when the marble is rolling down the ramp, its potential energy is changed into kinetic energy. When the marble hits the cup, the mechanical energy of the marble does work on the cup—it moves the cup!

> You can check out the relationship between kinetic and potential energy by looking at skateboards and ramps!
>
> PS
>
> 🔍 energy skate park basics 1.1

When you increase the mass of the marble or increase its starting height, you increase the mechanical energy of the marble, and it moves the cup farther. But if you decrease the mass of the marble or lower its starting height, the marble has less mechanical energy, and moves the cup a shorter distance.

In ballistics, mechanical energy is very important. The more energy you have, the higher, farther, and faster you can you throw, toss, and fire your projectiles. And for centuries, people have been building machines to do just that. Whether it's an atlatl, a bow, a catapult, or a gun, they all turn potential energy into kinetic energy to send projectiles on their ballistic trajectories.

A catapult at Castelnaud Castle in France. This site from the Middle Ages has many re-creations of weapons that were used in past centuries.

SLINGSHOTS

Have you ever stretched out a rubber band only to have it snap back on your hand? Ouch! The energy in the band to snap your fingers happens when the elastic potential energy of the stretched rubber band is turned into kinetic energy. Slingshots also use elastic potential energy to fire projectiles on ballistic trajectories.

Although they look like an old and simple tool, slingshots have been around only since the 1850s, when rubber was invented.

Simple slingshots can be made from a Y-shaped piece of wood or other sturdy material, with a strong but flexible elastic band stretched between the upper parts of the Y. When someone grips the bottom of the Y as a handle, the elastic band can be pulled back to increase its potential energy and then released to convert it to kinetic energy. Zing!

WORDS TO KNOW

longbow: a wooden bow drawn by hand.

BOWS AND ARROWS

Slingshots are not the only things that use elastic energy to power projectiles. The bow and arrow, one of the most ancient tools of hunters and soldiers, is still popular today. From the tales of Robin Hood to *The Hunger Games*, archery has appeared in legends and stories old and new.

The tools of an archer can be different depending on their history and purpose, but the basic parts are the same. All bows consist of two main parts: the bow and the bow string. When the bow string is drawn back, the bow bends, increasing the elastic potential energy of the bow. When the bow string is released, it snaps back. As the potential energy from the bow is converted to kinetic energy, it moves the bow string and the arrow, quickly accelerating the arrow to its target.

The earliest evidence of archery comes from South Africa, where stone arrowheads dating back more than 64,000 years have been found in rock formations.

For ancient people, creating bows and arrows was a difficult process.

A strong but flexible wood was needed for the bow. A tough string, made of plant and animal fiber, needed to be strong enough to bend the bow without breaking. And carving straight arrows that flew well was a challenge of its own. As centuries passed, different cultures made their own sizes and shapes of bows and arrows, each designed to fit the needs of their unique cultures.

The Tale of Robin Hood

Have you heard of Friar Tuck or the Sheriff of Nottingham? The centuries-old stories of Robin Hood and his band of thieves are still told today. Supposedly, they stole from the rich to give to the poor. But was Robin Hood a real person?

PS Check out this site to learn more.

🔍 historic UK Robin Hood

Bows can come in many shapes and sizes, but three types are the most common. The **longbow** is the simplest kind of bow, used by different cultures and peoples around the world. The longbow was used for hunting, sports, and in battle, especially during the Middle Ages.

The English were very successful using the longbow, and it's featured in many English tales and legends, including Robin Hood.

DID YOU KNOW?

Smaller versions of the longbow are called short bows. They are mostly used today to teach archery to beginners.

Longbows were usually big, around 4 to 5 feet tall, and made of a strong but flexible yew wood. During battles in the Middle Ages, hundreds of archers would fire with longbows at once, raining deadly arrows down on their enemies from great distances.

Battle of Crécy between the English and French in the Hundred Years' War

Jean Froissart (1337–1410)

This painting shows bowmen fighting a battle with longbows. What other devices can you spot that use projectiles?

WORDS TO KNOW

recurve bow: a bow with limbs that curve away from the archer when unstrung.

compound bow: a bow that uses a levering system, often cables and pulleys, to bend the limbs.

mechanical advantage: the amount a machine multiplies a force to make a task easier.

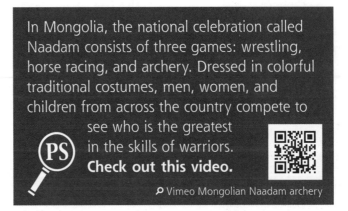

In Mongolia, the national celebration called Naadam consists of three games: wrestling, horse racing, and archery. Dressed in colorful traditional costumes, men, women, and children from across the country compete to see who is the greatest in the skills of warriors. **Check out this video.**

🔎 Vimeo Mongolian Naadam archery

The **recurve bow** is smaller than the longbow, which makes it easier to carry and shoot. Recurve bows were first used in Mongolia, where riders on horseback found that its smaller size made it easier to shoot while on the move. You might think that a smaller bow would be less powerful, but its shape helps make up for its difference in size.

The word "recurve" comes from the extra curve of the bow, which bends back on itself. This extra curve stops the string earlier and quicker than the longbow, delivering more energy to the arrow. Today, recurve bows are used in many archery competitions, including the Olympic Games.

Gwen Sheppard uses a recurve bow during the archery competition of the 2012 Warrior Games. Sheppard is with the Air Force team.
credit: U.S. Air Force/Val Gempis

U.S. Invictus team archer Chasity Kuczer competes with a compound bow at the 2016 Invictus Games.

credit: DoD News photo by EJ Hersom (CC BY 2.0)

Recurve bows and longbows are excellent tools for launching arrows, but they both need a lot of strength and stamina to use—which can quickly tire out archers. The **compound bow** is designed to lessen the amount of strength an archer needs. Compound bows use pulleys to help increase the energy delivered to the arrow while requiring less strength to draw the string back.

> **Thanks to this mechanical advantage, compound bows can be smaller than both longbows and recurve bows, while still firing arrows with even greater force and accuracy.**

Slingshots and bows are great for hitting targets with precision, but their projectiles are small. What if you want to send something bigger on a ballistic trajectory? What would happen if you tried to launch a bowling ball with a slingshot or put a basketball on the tip of an arrow? The laws of motion say that to accelerate a bigger mass, you need a greater force. So what kind of machine can throw heavy things great distances? Catapults!

WORDS TO KNOW

engineer: a person who uses math, science, and creativity to solve problems or meet human needs.

fortification: a walled-in area to protect against an enemy.

mangonel: a military device for throwing stones and other projectiles.

biological warfare: the use of toxins or other biological matter as weapons.

payload: the object or load that is being delivered by the catapult.

torsion: a twisting force that turns or twirls a material.

tension: a pulling force that pulls or stretches an object.

SIEGE ENGINES: THE CATAPULTS

In the Middle Ages, stone walls were used to protect kingdoms and castles from invaders. Castles were built with especially thick stone walls and were sometimes surrounded by moats and other traps to keep armies from approaching. Archers often lined the tops of the walls, ready to rain down arrows on anyone who got too close. Attacking forces would lay siege to these well-defended places, often surrounding the towns and castles just outside their walls. But castles were often filled with food and supplies, and the people inside would try to wait out any attack if the walls held.

This gave **engineers** a difficult problem to solve. If archers and swordsmen couldn't break through a wall, what could be done? The answer was to build siege engines. Siege engines are machines built to help forces break through walls—or go over them. One effective and deadly siege engine was the catapult.

Catapults are large machines that toss heavy objects such as boulders, spears, and even fireballs on ballistic trajectories at and over enemy **fortifications**. If an attacking army had catapults, it could possibly break through even the thickest walls. If that failed, it could use the catapults to send crushing stones and fire raining down on people inside the walls. One of the most common catapults is called a **mangonel**.

DID YOU KNOW?

The catapults you might have seen in pictures or movies were the kinds first used in the Middle Ages, but similar machines were used thousands of years ago by the Chinese, Greeks, Romans, and others. Like archery, catapults were used by many cultures around the world.

Biological Warfare

Catapults weren't used only to heave heavy stones or fireballs. Sometimes, they were used to spread disease. In 1346, while laying siege to the city of Caffa, the Mongol army used catapults to hurl plague-infected corpses over the city walls. The bubonic plague, also called the Black Death, spread quickly and killed thousands who had no escape from the surrounding Mongol armies. The survivors fleeing the siege spread the plague into Europe. Catapult-spread plague is one of the earliest examples of **biological warfare**.

MANGONEL

The mangonel was first used by the Romans around 400 BCE. Mangonels have a long arm with a bowl-shaped platform on one end to hold the **payload**. The arm is attached to an axle, which is wound with many ropes. To prepare the mangonel to fire, the arm is slowly pulled back, twisting the ropes around the axle, creating **torsion**. This can produce a lot of potential energy.

When the arm is released, the tension in the ropes causes the arm to snap back with tremendous force until it is stopped by a crossbar, and the projectile is thrown toward the target.

The most powerful mangonels could fire projectiles more than 1,300 feet. They were often built on wheels, making them easier to move around in battle. **Check out a working mangonel here!**

PS

🔍 Mangonel Artillery Snow

The launch angle can be changed by raising or lowering the crossbar. This allows the crew to change the ballistic path of the projectile.

WORDS TO KNOW

missile: an object or weapon that is propelled toward a target.

counterweight: a weight that balances another weight.

fulcrum: the point on which a lever rests or is supported and on which it pivots.

ballista: a large crossbow for firing a spear. Plural is ballistae.

Mangonels have a few disadvantages. The stretching and twisting of their ropes can cause them to weaken and break over time, making them less accurate. A stronger and more accurate type of catapult is the trebuchet.

The earliest trebuchets are thought to have been made in China around 300 BCE. Like the mangonel, a trebuchet has a long arm used to throw projectiles with great force. But instead of using torsion to power their **missiles**, trebuchets use gravitational potential energy.

DID YOU KNOW?

Some of the things people used as projectiles with mangonels included burning sand, dead animals, feces, sharp wooden poles, and vats of burning tar.

These trebuchets were reconstructed at Castelnaud Castle.

A trebuchet has a long arm, or lever, attached to a heavy **counterweight**. The arm moves around a **fulcrum**, which is closer to one end than the other. The counterweight is attached to the shorter end of the lever, and the payload is held in a pouch and a sling attached to the longer side.

To fire the trebuchet, the long end of the arm is pulled down, lifting the counterweight into the air. This gives the trebuchet a lot of gravitational potential energy. While the arm is held in place, the projectile is loaded into a sling. When the arm is released, the counterweight drops, the arm whips through the air, and the payload is launched with great speed toward its target.

Punkin Chunkin

Catapults, like mangonels and trebuchets, have been around for centuries. But just because they're old doesn't mean they aren't fun! There are competitions around the world to see who can fling objects the greatest distance using these ancient technologies. One of the most popular projectiles is a pumpkin!

Watch this video on the science behind "punkin chunkin!"

PS

🔎 YouTube physics punkin chunkin

Because gravity pulls on the counterweight with the same amount of force every time, trebuchets are more accurate than the rope-twisting mangonel, and they don't break as often!

The word trebuchet comes from the French word *trebucher*, meaning "over throw."

Trebuchets are very good at lofting heavy stones and other deadly projectiles to great heights, making them especially useful for throwing things over towering defenses. But they weren't very useful for nearby foes. Instead, many armies used the **ballista** when opposing forces came too close.

BALLISTAE

One of the deadliest types of catapult was the ballista. Ballistae are like **crossbows**, but much larger. These lethal weapons were fired almost straight ahead into the charging enemy.

Ballistae use torsion and tension to power projectiles. Two wooden arms are attached to ropes, which are twisted together and drawn back. Once the string is locked into place, large arrows or bolts are loaded into the center track and aimed at the target. With the release of the bow string, the ropes unwind, propelling the deadly projectile at the enemy.

Mangonels, trebuchets, and ballistae are just a few of the many different catapults that were used for centuries. They were often built on wheels so they could be moved into just the right position. They dominated battlefields until a more powerful weapon came along: firearms.

Did you know that catapults are still used by the military? Aircraft carriers use steam-powered catapults to launch planes from 0 to 165 miles per hour in just two seconds! **You can watch a video of these catapult systems here.**

PS

ENG Aircraft carrier catapult

FIREARMS

Compared to modern guns, the first firearms were not very good. The earliest examples, called fire lances, were made in tenth-century China. Fire lances were long tubes made of bamboo filled with an early form of gunpowder. They were dangerous, but not very accurate. They were just as likely to explode as they were to hit their target.

DID YOU KNOW?

Although they might resemble a rifle, BB guns and air rifles aren't really firearms. Instead of using a chemical reaction, they use compressed air to send a BB or pellet at a target.

Firearms all work in the same basic way. A projectile, called a **bullet**, sits inside a **barrel**. But instead of using elastic or gravitational potential energy, firearms use **chemical potential energy**. When gunpowder is ignited, gases expand very quickly inside the barrel, converting the potential energy into kinetic energy and pushing the projectile out of the barrel at an incredible speed.

As the technology of firearms spread around the world, weapons such as cannons and muskets replaced catapults and archers in battle. Stone walls were no match for the violence and destruction of a heavy cannonball fired at high speed.

Bullets are some of the fastest projectiles around. The quickest can achieve speeds of 1,700 miles per hour, more than twice the speed of sound. It's this speed that gives dangerous weapons such as cannons, mortars, and guns their range and power. The ability of modern guns and rifles to cause harm and destruction makes them a very **controversial** topic around the world.

Now that you know how projectiles are launched in the air, we'll look at some of the things these projectiles can do while they're up there!

ESSENTIAL QUESTION

Why do people keep inventing new and improved ways of sending projectiles through the air?

ATLATL BATTLE

Different kinds of spear-throwing tools were used by ancient people around the world, but they all worked in the same basic way. It takes a lot of practice to use an atlatl, but you can make your own and try it out at home!

> **Warning:** Never point or fire any weapon at a living creature and always wear eye protection. Ask an adult to help with the knife in this activity.

❯ **Attach one binder clip to one end of the ruler.** This is the "spur." Fold the clip handles back.

❯ **Using a small knife, CAREFULLY carve a notch into the eraser of each pencil.** The notch should go about half way into the eraser and be wide enough to fit onto the binder clip handle. The pencils will be your darts.

❯ **Place an eraser cap on the unsharpened end of the pencil.** This will help your dart fly and be much safer!

❯ **Place the binder handle into the notch in the eraser** and lay the pencil onto the ruler lengthwise.

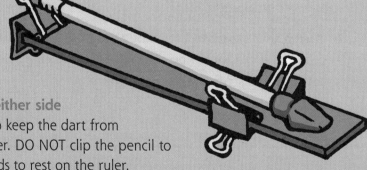

❯ **Attach binder clips on either side of the pencil.** These will help keep the dart from sliding off the sides of the ruler. DO NOT clip the pencil to the ruler. The pencil only needs to rest on the ruler.

> In a safe and open space, hold the ruler at the end opposite the spur. Don't hold onto the pencil! It should only rest on the ruler.

> Keeping the ruler flat and level so the dart can't slide out, reach back, and quickly bring the ruler forward like you're throwing a paper airplane. Turn your wrist down at the end of the motion. Don't let go of the ruler!

> What happened? Was the motion what you expected? Using an atlatl takes a lot of patience and practice!

If you're having trouble getting the right motion, check out this video on how to throw using an atlatl!

(PS)

🔎 YouTube simple atlatl

Questions to think about

* How is the atlatl a machine?

* What forces are acting on the dart as it's thrown?

* What forces are acting on it once it's released?

* What other motions are like the one you use to throw the dart?

Try This!

Try hitting a target! How accurate can you be? What might make your dart more accurate? How far can you throw? Try comparing the atlatl to simply throwing your dart. Which gives you greater range?

Does adding weight to the dart or the atlatl make a difference? Try making a larger atlatl to throw even larger darts. How far can you throw?

SLING TIME!

Modern slingshots use special elastic materials and different shapes to give shooters even more accuracy and power. But you can make your own!

> **Warning:** Never point or fire a slingshot or any other weapon at a living creature. Always wear eye protection.

> **Cut two rubber bands into single strips** of the same length.

> **Tie the first rubber band to one branch of the Y and the second rubber band to the other branch.** Be sure to tie them tightly! If you need to, secure them to branches of the Y using tape.

> **Out of leather or sturdy cloth, cut a rectangular pouch to hold your projectiles.** Cut or punch two holes on either side of the pouch.

> **Tie a rubber band to each hole in the pouch** and reinforce them with tape.

> **Find a large, open space outdoors to test your slingshot.** Place your projectile in the pouch and launch it! Aim at an appropriate target, such as a piece of paper or a tin can.

> **Challenge your friends to a contest.** Who is the best shot?

Questions to think about

* When is the potential energy the greatest?

* When is the kinetic energy the greatest?

* How does the mass of your projectile affect its flight?

* What forces are acting on your projectile before you let go?

* What forces are acting on your projectile once it's fired?

Activity

Try This!

Try adding more rubber bands to your slingshot. How do more rubber bands affect the mechanical energy of the slingshot and projectile? What's the farthest you can fire a projectile with your slingshot?

Consider This!

Using a slingshot can get pretty tiring for your hands, especially the one holding the tool. Some slingshots are designed with a brace that goes around the wrist of the hand holding the slingshot. This adds support and increases the amount of strength you can use to stretch that elastic back. How can you add wrist support to the slingshot you just made? How does this affect your shot?

BUILD A MANGONEL

Mangonels use tension and torsion to fling their projectiles great distances. But you don't need a medieval army to build one for you—you can make your own at home!

> **Warning:** Never point or fire a mangonel or any other weapon at a living creature. Always wear eye protection.

❯ **Stack at least five craft sticks together.** Tightly wrap both ends with rubber bands and set aside.

❯ **Stack two craft sticks together.** Tightly wrap one end with rubber bands.

❯ **Carefully separate the stack of two craft sticks.** Put the stack of five craft sticks between the two craft sticks.

❯ **Slide the stack of five craft sticks close to the rubber-banded end of the two craft sticks.** Wrap at least one rubber band around both stacks of craft sticks to secure them together.

❯ **Glue and tape a plastic spoon** to the end of the top craft stick. Place your projectile in the spoon.

❯ **Push down on the top craft stick and release!** You might need to hold your mangonel down. When you push down on the stick, you're loading the mangonel with potential energy. When you let go, that potential energy becomes kinetic energy, sending the projectile on its way! The more potential energy you put into the catapult, the greater the kinetic energy—and the farther it will fly!

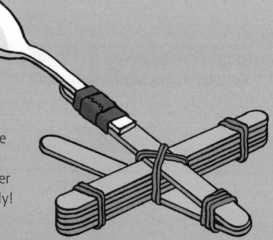

Questions to think about

* What kind of catapult is this?

* What kind of potential energy does your catapult use?

* What affects how far and how high you can catapult your projectile?

* How accurate is your catapult?

* What's the highest your catapult can launch a projectile?

* How would you measure it?

* What's the farthest your catapult can fire?

Consider This!

How can you change the launch angle of your catapult? What happens if you change the length of the throwing arm? Can you design a different or better catapult using the same materials?

Brutal Battle

During the Siege of Lisbon in the twelfth century, English crusaders attacked the Muslim city of Lisbon in the country of Portugal. The siege lasted four months and was successful at least partly because of the use of mangonels. It's said that the English worked in teams of 100 men who used two mangonels to throw 5,000 rocks in 10 hours! Once the Muslims had surrendered, the terms dictated that the Crusaders would allow the people to keep their lives and possessions, but these terms were broken as the Crusaders entered the city and killed the inhabitants or drove them away.

BUILD A TREBUCHET

Trebuchets use gravity to send their cargo flying. If you've got a castle to invade, it might be the siege weapon for you!

> **Warning:** Never point or fire a trebuchet or any other weapon at a living creature. Always wear eye protection.

> First, build two A-shaped braces.

* Cut one craft stick in half. Use two long sticks and one half-stick to make each A shape.

* At the top of the A, the two long sticks should cross each other and make a small v. This is where the pencil will sit. Glue the craft sticks where they meet.

* Repeat for the other brace.

* Stand up one brace on the cardboard and mark where the legs are.

* Cut slots into the cardboard to fit the legs of the brace. Use other craft sticks, glue, or tape to reinforce the brace on the cardboard.

* Do the same for the other brace. The braces should be a few inches apart, wide enough that a pencil can rest across both of them.

> Then, build the arm.

* Cut two small notches across from each other at one end of one craft stick. These should be wide enough to fit a piece of string.

* Make a loop of string about 1 to 1½ inches long. Tape one end of the loop to a battery.

* Hang the other end of the loop through the notches on the craft stick. Tape or glue the string to the notches.

* Open one end of a paper clip to make a hook, leaving the rest of the paper clip flat.

* Tape the flat part of the paper clip to the craft stick opposite the battery. The hook should point up and away from the battery.

> Next, build the pivot.

* Cut off a 1-inch piece of plastic straw. Using tape or rubber bands, attach the straw to the arm, perpendicular to it. The straw should be closer to the battery than the paper clip.

* Slide the pencil through the straw and lay the pencil across the braces so it rests in the small v at the top.

* Attach the pencil to the braces using tape or rubber bands. The arm should pivot around the straw.

> Finally, prepare the sling and payload.

* Make a loop of string about 1 to 1½ inches long.

* Use tape to attach your small projectile to the string.

* Hang the loop on the paperclip hook.

> Fire your trebuchet! Pull down on your payload and release!

Questions to think about

* What kind of potential energy is used by the trebuchet?

* How is the potential energy turned into kinetic energy?

* How does the sling affect the flight of the projectile?

* What affects the launch angle of your payload?

* What's the farthest you can fling a projectile?

Try This!

Try counterweights other than the battery. How does the weight affect the flight of the projectile? What happens if you change the arm? Try moving the pivot point. What happens? What about making the arm longer or shorter?

GET ENERGIZED!

Potential energy and kinetic energy are closely related. You can see the effects of both in this experiment.

❯ **Turn a plastic or paper cup upside down** and cut an opening at the lip big enough for your marbles to fit through.

❯ **Place a cardboard tube at an angle,** taping one end to the floor and one end to a sturdy object such as a table leg or a wall. Be sure that your marble can easily roll through the tube!

❯ **Place the cup upside down** at the bottom of the tube with the opening facing the tube so that the cup will catch the marble. Don't tape the cup to floor.

❯ **Place one marble at the top of the tube, and let it roll!** How far does it move the cup? Measure and record the data in your engineering notebook. Do this several times with the same marble. Can you average the distance?

❯ **Repeat the experiment with marbles or balls of different weights.** Record how far each ball moves the cup.

Questions to think about

* When is the marble's potential energy the greatest?

* When is the marble's kinetic energy the greatest?

* Which marble has the greatest potential energy?

* Which marble has the greatest kinetic energy?

* Where are the kinetic and potential energy equal?

* How does the marble's mass affect the movement of the cup?

Try This!

Change the height of the tube and repeat the experiment. How does it change the mechanical energy of the marble? How does it affect the motion of the cup?

Chapter 4

CURVEBALLS AND SPIRALS:
AIR RESISTANCE

Pitchers throw curveballs, making batters swing wildly. Football players throw perfect spirals, the balls spinning rapidly as they land in the arms of receivers. And skydivers hang below parachutes, drifting slowly to Earth.

We've learned that the only force acting on a ballistic object is gravity. But that's not completely true! There's something else: air. Fortunately for us, we live on a planet with an **atmosphere**. It protects us from harmful **radiation** and gives us oxygen to breath. But the air also affects projectiles in weird and interesting ways.

Remember Galileo's experiment atop the leaning tower of Pisa? Suppose you were to drop a feather and bowling ball at the same time. According to Galileo's experiment, they should hit the ground at the same time.

ESSENTIAL QUESTION

What are some different ways of manipulating the motion of a projectile through the air, and why are these useful?

WORDS TO KNOW

atmosphere: the mixture of gases surrounding Earth.

radiation: energy transmitted in the form of rays, waves, or particles from a source, such as the sun.

drag: the force air exerts on a body moving through it.

surface area: a measure of the total area that the surface of an object occupies.

aeronautical engineer: a person who designs and tests aircraft.

aerodynamic: having a shape that reduces the amount of drag created by air passing around or over it.

streamlined: designed with a smooth surface that minimizes resistance through air or water

But do they? If they don't, does it mean Galileo was wrong? Or is something else going on?

Imagine standing on a chair and dropping a flat piece of paper and a crumpled piece of paper at the same time. Do they hit the ground together? The two pieces of paper have the same mass, but they fall at different rates. According to Galileo, that shouldn't happen!

Is gravity really affecting the two objects differently, or is there some other force at work?

The flat piece of paper is experiencing more **drag,** or air resistance. Air resistance is the force of friction between an object and the air it's moving through. The amount of air resistance on a projectile depends on the projectile's size and speed. When you drop a flat piece of paper, it has a lot of **surface area** facing the direction it's traveling.

A Feather on the Moon

What would happen if you repeated the paper experiment on the moon? During one of his moonwalks, *Apollo 15* commander David Scott (1932–) demonstrated Galileo's discovery by dropping a feather and a hammer at the same time.

 What do you think happened? **You can check out Scott's amazing experiment here!**

🔎 NASA hammer feather

This creates a lot of drag, slowing the paper's acceleration. The crumpled paper experiences drag, too, but the amount of air resistance is less because the paper has a smaller surface area in the direction it's moving.

For most things, including slingshots and basketballs, air resistance is so small that it can be ignored. But when objects are really big or move very fast, even a little bit of surface area can create a lot of drag and change their ballistic trajectories.

DID YOU KNOW?

Aerodynamics is a part of physics that studies how air moves around things such as airplane wings and rockets. Scientists who study aerodynamics to design better and more efficient airplanes are called **aeronautical engineers**.

To lessen the amount of air resistance, things such as arrows, airplanes, rockets, and even cars are designed to be more **aerodynamic** or **streamlined**. The more streamlined a projectile is, the less drag it has—and the farther and faster it can fly!

Although making objects more aerodynamic can help them reach amazing speeds, sometimes slowing a projectile down is important, too.

PARACHUTES

While most things that move through the air try to keep the amount of drag as small as possible, lots of air resistance can sometimes be very helpful. Suppose you wanted to deliver something fragile by firing it from a cannon or dropping it from an airplane? It probably wouldn't survive its flight unless you could find a way to slow it down before it's smashed to bits.

Parachutes are used to deliver important supplies to hard-to-reach places and softly return astronauts to Earth. How do they work?

In the 1470s, the famous artist and inventor Leonardo da Vinci (1452–1519) designed a "tented roof" to carry a person underneath it. There's no record of it ever being tested, but many historians consider it the first parachute!

Instead of having a streamlined shape, parachutes are large and open. They're designed with lots of surface area. This lets them catch as much air as possible and create a lot of air resistance as they fall.

By pushing against so much air, parachutes use the force of drag to slow down and safely land payloads such as space capsules and skydivers.

Jump!

Alan Eustace (1957–) is an engineer who holds the record for the highest jump back to Earth. He rose more than 135,000 feet attached to a balloon, and then jumped back to Earth with a parachute.

 You can listen to his TED Talk at this website.

🔍 Eustace TED

And watch a video of him at this website.

🔍 Guardian Eustace

When skydivers leap from airplanes, they experience air resistance as they fall to Earth. As the force of gravity accelerates the skydiver, Earth's atmosphere pushes back. When the force of drag equals the force of gravity, the skydiver no longer accelerates. This is called **terminal velocity**. A skydiver reaches terminal velocity at about 125 miles per hour!

But parachutes aren't the only things that use air resistance and drag in interesting ways. There are other projectiles that can use these powerful forces.

THROWING A CURVE

A batter swings at a pitch, only to watch it curve under the bat at the last second. A striker scores a spectacular goal, and the replay shows the fantastic shot curling past the goalie's outstretched hands into the back of the net. How does this happen?

Dick Rudolph (1887–1949), who was known for throwing curveballs, used this grip on the ball.

credit: Library of Congress

optical illusion: a trick of the eyes that makes people see something differently than it really is.

turbulent: unsteady or violent movement.

Magnus effect: when air pressure on one side of a ball is greater than on the other side, making the ball move toward the side where there is less pressure.

After a ball is thrown or kicked, it follows a ballistic trajectory, with gravity and air resistance the only forces acting on it. Newton's first law says that an object needs a force to change speed or direction, so how do baseballs and soccer balls manage to curve?

For years, people thought that curve balls in sports were a trick of the eye, used to fool the other team. Is a curve ball an optical illusion or is it real?

A special kind of ball can help us sort this out—the Wiffle ball. How does a Wiffle ball move through the air? Instead of flying steadily like a baseball or tennis ball, it wiggles and waggles its way across the field. You can see for yourself by doing the activity on page 90.

The holes of the Wiffle ball are important to its wild turns and sudden wobbles. As air flows over and through the holes, it becomes **turbulent**. Because the air doesn't flow smoothly around the ball, the air resistance is unequal on different parts of the ball. And thanks to Newton's first law, we know that unbalanced forces can cause things to change direction or speed. When the Wiffle ball is thrown, these unbalanced forces cause the ball to curve, dip, and dive dramatically!

DID YOU KNOW?

The Wiffle ball was originally created out of perfume packaging! In 1953, a dad named David Mullany used a razor blade to slice holes into a hard plastic ball so his son could make balls serve and curve with ease.

And it turns out that you don't need holes to make projectiles move in strange ways—you can do it with spin!

CURVEBALLS AND CURLED KICKS

When a pitcher throws a curveball, they grip the ball in such a way that it spins very quickly when it's released toward home plate. As the ball spins, a thin layer of air spins with it.

As the ball sails toward the plate, it runs into air pushing it in the opposite direction.

The thin layer of air speeds up the oncoming air on one side of the ball but slows it down on the other. This causes a difference in pressure on either side of the ball, pushing the ball in the direction of its spin.

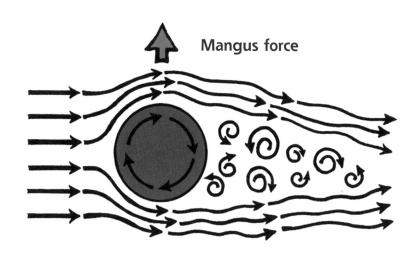

Mangus force

Different grips and kicks can spin balls in different ways, making balls curve left, right, and even up or down! This is called the **Magnus effect**, and it gives curveballs their curve, causes golf balls to slice, and lets soccer players' shots seem to avoid the goalkeeper on their way into the back of the net!

When you throw or toss something, you usually can't help but give it a little spin. Athletes who put a lot of spin on balls can make their sport's projectiles do some amazing things.

Check out this video of a soccer player using the

PS Magnus effect to curl a ball into the goal!

🔎 Physics Girl magnus

But have you wondered what can happen when there's no spin on a ball?

KNUCKLING

Have you heard of a **knuckleball**? In baseball, only a few pitchers have mastered the knuckleball's unpredictable movements. Unlike other pitches, knuckleballs are thrown so that the ball has as little spin as possible.

The result is a pitch that moves in ways that make it hard for a batter to hit, and difficult for a catcher to catch!

So how does it work? Scientists aren't completely sure. Researchers think that as a knuckleball is thrown, the stitches on the baseball's surface cause turbulence in the thin layer of air around the ball. But unlike with a curveball, this turbulence causes forces to push the knuckleball in different directions instead of one.

Good Pitchin'

Have you heard of R.A. Dickey (1974–)? In 2012, he won the Cy Young baseball award as the best pitcher in the National League. His knuckleballs are amazing to watch!

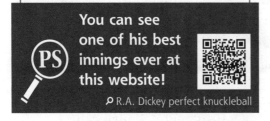

You can see one of his best innings ever at this website!

🔎 R.A. Dickey perfect knuckleball

This strange knuckling effect is also seen in soccer, when a ball is kicked so that it has very little spin. But soccer balls don't have stitches sticking out the way baseballs do, so there must be something else going on. Maybe you'll be the person to figure it out!

In many sports, spin is used to change the ballistic trajectory of projectiles. But spin can also keep a projectile headed in the right direction.

TOUCHDOWN!

Do you watch or play American football? A football has an interesting shape. Instead of being round like a soccer ball, it's wide in the middle and pointed on both ends.

Good quarterbacks can throw footballs incredible distances with amazing accuracy. But if you tried to throw a football without practice, it probably wouldn't get very far.

Inexperienced players can get frustrated as the ball tumbles end over end as soon as it leaves their hand. So how do football players make it look so easy?

DID YOU KNOW?

The mathematical name for the shape of an American football is a "prolate spheroid." Playing a game of prolate spheroid would sound a little strange. No wonder they just call it a football!

Just like a baseball pitcher, quarterbacks spin the ball as it leaves their hands. This is called "throwing a **spiral**."

WORDS TO KNOW

axis: an imaginary line down the middle of a sphere around which it rotates.

angular momentum: an object's resistance to either start or stop spinning due to inertia.

gyroscope: a spinning wheel or disk used to measure or maintain orientation.

orientation: the direction and position of something compared to something else.

gyroscopic stabilization: when a spinning object stays pointed in the direction it was thrown.

fletching: feather-like material at the end of an arrow.

To throw a spiral, the player must spin the football around an imaginary line called an **axis** that connects its two pointy ends. Throwing a spiral is not easy—it takes a lot of practice to throw the perfect spiral like a professional football player. Even the best athletes can struggle to throw it correctly! So why do they throw it in such a difficult way?

In baseball, pitchers put spin on the ball to make it harder to hit. But in football, quarterbacks put spin on the ball to make it easier to catch! That's because a spinning football has **angular momentum**.

According to Newton's first law, when something is in motion, it resists changing its motion due to its inertia.

What's a Gyroscope?

Because spinning objects resist a change in their orientation, they can be made to do all kinds of interesting things. A **gyroscope** can be easily balanced on a string or the tip of a finger and is even used to help airplanes and spacecraft know which way they're pointed!

credit: Misko (CC by 2.0)

 (PS) **Check out this video to learn more about gyroscopes!**

🔎 ScienceOnline gyroscope

That happens with spinning objects, too! When you spin a top, it wants to keep spinning the same way and resists falling over. As a football spins around its axis, it acts like a top and resists any change in its **orientation**. That means the ball stays pointed in the direction it's thrown. This is called **gyroscopic stabilization**.

A well-thrown spiral makes the football less wobbly and it also makes it more aerodynamic. Maybe more importantly, it also makes the ball much easier for someone to catch!

If a football is thrown without spin, it can tumble end over end. That tumbling makes it really hard to catch a last-minute, game-winning touchdown pass!

Gyroscopic stabilization isn't used just by quarterbacks and archers, however. It turns out that bullets spin, too.

DID YOU KNOW?

In archery, arrows are designed to spin, too. At the rear of the arrow, feather-like material called **fletching** is made with a slight twist. This causes the arrow to spin as it flies and increases the archer's accuracy!

THE RIFLE

The earliest bullets were small metal balls that bounced around inside the gun barrel, making their trajectories unpredictable. **Marksmen** had to be close to their targets to be sure they could hit their marks. Otherwise, chances were good that they'd miss!

In the sixteenth century, an important improvement made guns much more accurate. The carving of grooves on the inside of a gun's barrel made it much easier for a marksman to strike a target, and do so from a far greater distance. As the bullet traveled along the barrel, the grooves gave the projectile spin—just like a spiral pass from a quarterback! This technique was called rifling, and it's how the rifle got its name.

DID YOU KNOW?

The first widespread use of modern, streamlined bullets in battle was during the American Civil War (1861–1865).

These are bullets from a Civil War battle found in the ground of Fredericksburg, Virginia.

The Gun Regulation Debate

In all recent wars, firearms such as guns and rifles have played a large part in battles, big and small. Firearms are also a controversial topic in many countries. Some countries have strict laws limiting who can own firearms and what kind they can own. In the United States, the Second Amendment to the U.S. Constitution states:

"A well regulated Militia, being necessary to the security of a free State, the right of the people to keep and bear Arms, shall not be infringed."

Many Americans believe the Second Amendment gives them the right to keep and own firearms without limits, while others argue that the writers of the Constitution meant for these weapons to be restricted. It is a very controversial topic. What do you think?

Finally, in the nineteenth century, the bullet was given a cone-like shape, making it more aerodynamic. All these improvements made rifles even more accurate—and deadlier.

Although they've advanced a lot in the last century, the basic design and physics behind firearms and bullets has stayed the same.

For most projectiles, thinking about drag or orientation isn't necessary. But the bigger and faster the projectile, the more important these elements become. Rockets are just about the biggest and fastest projectiles there are! We'll learn about these machines in the next chapter.

ESSENTIAL QUESTION

What are some different ways of manipulating the motion of a projectile through the air, and why are these useful?

GALILEO'S EXPERIMENT, PART 3

When you first did Galileo's famous experiment, you saw that gravity pulls on everything the same way, causing things such as tennis balls and dump trucks to fall at the same rate and hit the ground at the same time. The second time, you used it to prove that horizontal and vertical motion are independent. Now you're going to put a wrinkle into the same experiment one more time—using paper!

▶ Take two pieces of paper and crumple one into a ball. Leave the other flat.

▶ Hold the flat piece of paper in one hand parallel to the ground. Hold the crumpled piece of paper in the other hand.

▶ At the same time, drop both the crumpled and the flat paper pieces of paper. What happens? Record your observations in your engineering notebook.

Questions to think about

* Compare the motions of the two pieces of paper. How are they different?

* Use a timer to record the rate of fall for each piece of paper. How can you explain the differences?

* What forces are affecting the motion of the pieces of paper?

* What would Newton and Galileo say about this experiment?

Try This!

Does holding the flat piece of paper vertically change how it falls? Can you fold or shape the paper in a different way to cause it to fall at a different rate? Try dropping an object that's the same size and shape as a sheet of paper (such as a large book) along with a single flat sheet. How do they compare?

BUILD YOUR OWN PARACHUTE

Do you have an important payload you want to deliver by slingshot, catapult, rocket, or just a hard throw? Then you might need a parachute to help it land!

❯ For the parachute, choose thin, light material to work with, such as cloth, paper, or plastic that can be cut. Cut your material into a circle.

❯ Cut at a least four evenly spaced, small holes around the edge of the parachute.

❯ Cut the same number of strings as holes. They should all be the same length.

❯ Tie a string to each hole. You might want to use tape to help reinforce the holes.

❯ Tie the strings together at the bottom and attach them to your payload. Use tape, glue, or another string.

❯ Test your parachute! Drop your payload from a safe height and see how it works. Does your valuable cargo survive?

Questions to think about

* How does the parachute keep the payload from falling as it normally would? What forces are at work?

* How does the mass of the payload affect the parachute?

* Does the height of the drop change how the parachute works?

Try This!

Try different shapes for your parachutes. Is there a best shape? Why or why not? Try placing a small hole in the center of your parachute. Does this affect how the parachute works?

WHAT MAKES WIFFLE BALLS WAFFLE?

Have you ever played Wiffle ball? The crazy plastic ball is famous for seeming to defy the laws of physics with its crazy curves and dramatic drops. What makes the Wiffle ball behave the way it does?

❯ **Wrap a few Wiffle balls with tape.** Try to use the same amount of tape for each ball. Cut through the tape of one Wiffle ball so that the holes are open but leave the other Wiffle balls covered.

❯ **Outdoors, throw one covered ball and the open ball several times each at a target.** Carefully observe how they move.

❯ **Try your best to throw each ball the same way,** and from the same distance. What happens? Draw the ballistic trajectory of each experiment in your engineering notebook.

Questions to think about

* Is there a difference in how the two balls move? If there is, what do you think is causing the difference? If not, why not?

* Why wrap the Wiffle balls with about the same amount of tape? And why try to throw them the same way each time?

Try This!

Try using something to throw the balls—a catapult or slingshot, for example. Does the way the projectiles are accelerated affect their motion? Try cutting the holes just on one side of one of the covered balls and throwing the ball with holes facing in different directions. Does this affect the ball's motion? Record the motion of the balls in slow-motion video and compare their trajectories. How do they differ? How are they the same? Can you think of ways to measure the differences using the camera?

TAKE IT FOR A SPIN

Football players make throwing a spiral look easy, but it certainly is not! So, why bother spinning a football in the first place? Is there something about spinning that helps quarterbacks throw those winning passes?

❯ Use a top or a fidget spinner if you have one, or make one yourself.

❯ To make your own top, glue a bead to a washer. The hole of the bead should be right over the center of the washer.

❯ Trim a bamboo skewer to about 2 inches long. Push the skewer through the washer and the hole in the bead, leaving about one-quarter of an inch sticking out of the bottom of the bead. Glue the skewer to the bead.

❯ Now, try to balance your top without spinning it. Can you do it?

❯ Spin it! What is the motion like? What observations can you make? What is it doing? What isn't it doing?

Questions to think about

* What do you notice about the motion of the top or spinner as it's spinning?

* Think about Newton's laws of motion. Can you use them to explain how the top keeps from falling over?

* What happens when it stops spinning?

* Does playing with your top or spinner give you any ideas as to why it might be helpful to spin a football when it's thrown?

Consider This!

What is important for something to spin like a top? Does the shape, weight, or size change how long it spins? Can you spin other objects like a top? Experiment with different materials to see what makes a good top or spinner.

CHUCK IT!

Throwing something like a football so that it spins isn't easy, but with practice you can do it!

❯ **Place your target in a wide-open space outside.** Give yourself at least 4 to 6 feet of space between you and the target.

❯ **Throw an empty paper towel roll at your target.** First, try throwing it without spin. Can you hit your target? Give yourself one point for each success.

❯ **Next, try spinning it along its length as you throw it.** This will take practice! Try rolling it off your fingers. Does spin help you hit your target? Give yourself two points each time you succeed.

Questions to think about

* What happened when the tube was thrown without spin? What was the motion like? Was it predictable? Were you able to hit the target?

* What happened when you spun the tube? What was the motion like this time? Did it make it easier or harder to hit the target than throwing the tube with no spin?

* Which is more accurate, throwing with or without spin?

* Explain your answer. Can you think of another example?

* What laws of motion are at work?

Try This!

Try your hand at throwing a football. It's not easy! What other projectiles can you spin?

Chapter 5

WHEN WHAT GOES UP DOESN'T COME DOWN:
ROCKETS

Have you ever watched a rocket launch? Months, sometimes even years, go into planning, all to come together for the countdown: 3 . . . 2 . . . 1 . . . BLAST OFF!

At first, rockets might not seem to have much in common with other projectiles, such as baseballs or bullets. Rockets are powerful and complicated machines that don't need a slingshot or a catapult to get them moving. And they can fly higher, faster, and farther than any other kind of projectile there is!

Rockets have sent space **probes** across the **solar system**, and even carried people to the moon and back. The same forces that shape the paths of balls and arrows work on rockets, too. And although rockets might seem like a recent invention, they've been around for a while—they're even older than the slingshot!

ESSENTIAL QUESTION

How are rockets similar to pebbles shot with a slingshot? How are they different?

WORDS TO KNOW

probe: a spaceship or other device used to explore outer space.

solar system: the collection of eight planets and their moons in orbit around the sun, together with smaller bodies in the form of asteroids, meteoroids, comets, and dwarf planets.

liquid-fueled rocket: a rocket that uses liquid propellants to create thrust.

propellant: a combination of fuel and oxidizer that burns to produce thrust in a rocket.

ballistic missile: a missile that is at first powered and guided but is then pulled by gravity to its target.

HISTORY OF ROCKETS

Rockets have been around a lot longer than you might think. For centuries, they were used as fireworks and weapons of war. The first rockets appeared in the thirteenth century, when the Chinese filled bamboo tubes with an early kind of gunpowder to create a fire lance.

Lighting these first rockets was very dangerous. Sometimes, the tubes would fly toward the enemy, but they were just as likely to explode in the hands of their creators.

DID YOU KNOW?

During the War of 1812, British forces used rockets during their attack on Fort McHenry. The attack inspired Francis Scott Key (1779–1843) to write a poem with the line "the rockets' red glare," which later became a line in "The Star-Spangled Banner."

As the use of rockets slowly spread to Europe and the Middle East, they were used in battles and wars, and were eventually replaced by more powerful firearms. The earliest rockets behaved more like fireworks, often scaring the enemy with flashes of light and a lot of noise. Despite the ability of rockets to occasionally fly to great heights, people didn't think of using rockets to explore space until the end of the nineteenth century.

Robert Goddard stands next to his **liquid-fueled rocket** in 1926.

credit: U.S. Air Force

In 1898, Russian schoolteacher Konstantin Tsiolkovsky (1857–1935) described how rockets might be used to reach space. He wrote that a rocket using a liquid fuel, such as kerosene, instead of a solid fuel, such as gunpowder, could carry rockets much higher than the only aircraft of the time—balloons. This idea excited people around the world, including an American named Robert Goddard (1882–1945). In 1926, Goddard launched the first rocket to use liquid **propellant**. While it flew to a height of only about 40 feet, it's considered the beginning of modern rocketry.

Goddard built and flew larger and more powerful rockets, even making a gyroscope system to help steer rockets in flight.

What did the first liquid-fueled rockets look like? **You can check out some of Robert Goddard's experiments with rockets here!**

PS

YouTube Goddard rockets

He used his rockets to study the atmosphere, and built a recovery system to bring his experiments safely to the ground by parachute.

The biggest advance in rocketry came during World War II with the invention of the first **ballistic missile**, the German V-2 rocket. The V-2 was a terrifying weapon. At its fastest, it could travel 3,500 miles per hour—faster than the speed of sound and much faster than any airplane of the time. The V-2 became the first manmade object to reach space.

A V-2 rocket
credit: U.S. Air Force

warhead: a weapon that is the explosive part of a missile.

Soviet Union: a country that existed from 1922 until 1991. Russia was part of the Soviet Union.

concentration camps: large camps where Jews and members of other groups were imprisoned by the Nazis during World War II. Prisoners were forced to perform hard labor and millions were killed.

artificial satellite: a man-made object that orbits the earth, moon, or other object.

antenna: a metal rod that sends and receives radio waves. Plural is antennae.

During flight, once its fuel was used up, the V-2 followed a ballistic trajectory to its target. It was capable of destroying an entire city block with its 2,000-pound **warhead**. The V-2's designer, Wernher von Braun (1912–1977), surrendered to the Americans at the end of the war and became an important part of the race between the United States and the **Soviet Union** to put a human on the moon.

These early rockets still couldn't travel very far. Just like other projectiles, they always fell back to Earth—or exploded. Although the V-2 could reach the edge of space, it couldn't stay there. To reach space, even more powerful rockets were needed.

DID YOU KNOW?

The term "rocket" can mean either the machine that carries people and things into space or the powerful engines used to get there!

Wernher von Braun

Despite his success building rockets, von Braun's membership in Germany's Nazi Party made him a controversial figure. To produce the V-2, the German Army relied on the slave labor of thousands of men and women held in **concentration camps**. Forced to work underground and in dangerous conditions, many thousands of people lost their lives constructing the new weapon. In fact, more people died building the V-2 than were killed by its use as a weapon. Although von Braun said he had no knowledge of the terrible working conditions, many historians doubt his claims.

Today's Space Exploration

Today, rocket flights might seem common, but getting to space is still very hard and very expensive. Private companies such as Space X and Blue Origin are making reusable rockets that can be flown many times, unlike most rockets in the past. Will these new rockets allow more people to catch a ride into space? What do you think?

 Check out the launch of SpaceX's *Falcon Heavy* and the landing of its two boosters!

🔎 SpaceX Falcon Heavy launch

Both the United States and the Soviet Union wanted to have the most powerful rockets in the world.

On October 4, 1957, the world was stunned when the Soviet Union launched the first **artificial satellite** into orbit. *Sputnik*, a small, silvery ball with a few radio **antennae**, circled the globe every 90 minutes! Just 12 years later, Neil Armstrong (1930–2012) and Buzz Aldrin (1930–) rode the massive Saturn V rocket into space and became the first people to walk on the moon!

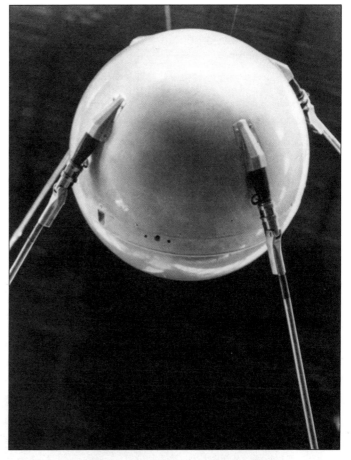

Sputnik, the world's first artificial satellite
credit: NASA

WORDS TO KNOW

hydrogen: a colorless, odorless, and flammable gas that is lighter than air.

oxidizer: a substance that contains oxygen, which mixes with fuel in a rocket engine to produce thrust.

liquid oxygen: a liquid produced by compressing oxygen gas.

combustion: a chemical reaction that produces heat and light.

combustion chamber: the part of a rocket where liquid fuel and oxidizer are combined to create a chemical reaction.

solid-fueled rocket: a rocket that uses solid propellants.

exhaust: the hot gases produced from a rocket's engine.

propel: to drive or move forward.

WHAT IS A ROCKET?

Rockets are different from catapults and rifles. Instead of using a separate machine to accelerate a projectile, rockets bring the machines along for the ride. Rockets regularly lift items such as satellites, space probes, and astronauts into space using powerful engines. These rocket engines provide a great amount of force to get their heavy payloads moving up and away from Earth. But how do rocket engines get things moving?

Just as with everything else, rockets use Newton's third law to get going. When you blow up a balloon, the air pushes against the inside rubber walls, keeping it inflated. But when the air is released, it rushes out in one direction, and the balloon shoots off in the opposite direction!

This force is called thrust, and it is the same force that carries rockets into space. It takes a lot of thrust to lift heavy things. To do this heavy lifting, rockets turn the chemical potential energy of rocket fuels into kinetic energy!

The Saturn V

The Saturn V was the largest rocket ever flown. It weighed 6.2 million pounds at liftoff and stood 363 feet tall. That's taller than a soccer field is long! At launch it generated 7.5 million pounds of thrust, which is more powerful than 85 Hoover Dams! The Saturn V took the *Apollo* astronauts to the moon!

 You can read more about the Saturn V and see pictures of its different parts in this infographic.

Space Saturn V infographic

A rocket blasting off. Now that's a lot of propulsion!
credit: NASA

PROPULSION

There are two main kinds of rocket engines. In a liquid-fueled rocket, a fuel, such as liquid **hydrogen**, is mixed with an **oxidizer**, such as **liquid oxygen**, in a **combustion chamber**, where they burn very quickly as soon as they meet. In a **solid-fueled rocket**, the fuel and oxidizer are mixed to make a solid propellant and carefully packed inside the rocket. When the propellant is ignited, it burns quickly at a very high heat.

Both kinds of rockets make extremely hot gases called **exhaust**. As the gases expand, they're expelled out of the rocket. Just like a loose balloon letting out air, the rocket is **propelled** in the opposite direction of the fiery and quick-moving exhaust, and we have liftoff!

DID YOU KNOW?

Because rocket engines apply force as the rocket climbs, the rocket is not really on a true ballistic trajectory when the engines are running! But once the engines are off, only gravity and air resistance affect the rocket's flight.

WORDS TO KNOW

stage: a smaller rocket that is stacked with other rockets and detaches when its fuel is used up.

jettison: to throw something away.

throttle: to control the amount of thrust.

booster: a rocket used to give another craft the power needed for takeoff.

The way rockets are accelerated is different from other projectiles. When an arrow or bullet is fired, a force is applied to accelerate them. But that force is only applied for a very brief instant. After that, they are on a ballistic trajectory. The only forces acting on them are gravity and a little air resistance.

For rockets to reach the speeds and heights needed to get into space, rocket engines apply a constant force to accelerate them.

By using rocket engines, spacecraft can accelerate gradually and safely on their way to space!

The rocket engines and the fuel to power them make rockets very heavy. In fact, most of a rocket's weight is fuel. To help them reach space, many rockets have separate parts called **stages**. Each rocket stage has its own engine and fuel. When a stage's fuel is all used up, the stage is **jettisoned**, and falls back to Earth. This makes the rest of the rocket lighter—and the less mass, the better!

Most rockets have two or three stages, or booster rockets, that fall away when their fuel is used up. This makes it easier for a rocket to reach the incredible speeds and heights needed to get to space.

PS Ride along with a space shuttle solid rocket booster from liftoff until it crashes back to Earth!

🔍 space shuttle rocket video

DID YOU KNOW?

Not all rockets discard their stages. The SpaceX Falcon 9's first stage can return to Earth and land under its own power! Check out this video to see two boosters land at once!

🔎 Falcon Heavy and Starman

A liquid-fueled rocket

A solid-fueled rocket

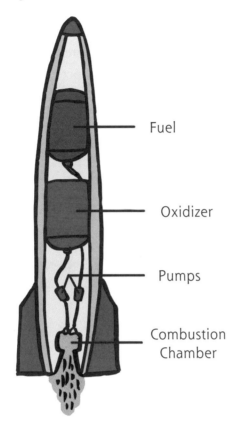

Fuel

Oxidizer

Pumps

Combustion
Chamber

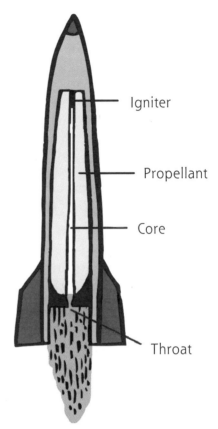

Igniter

Propellant

Core

Throat

Why Two Kinds of Rocket Engines?

Both liquid-fueled and solid-fueled rockets have advantages and disadvantages. Liquid-fueled rockets are very complicated, but they can be **throttled** up or down to change their amount of thrust. Solid-fueled rockets are very simple, but once they're ignited, they can't be turned off! Most rockets today use liquid-fueled rocket engines. Solid-fueled rockets are used mostly as **boosters**, which help lift the main rocket at the beginning of its flight. When they're used up, they separate from the main rocket and fall back to Earth.

WORDS TO KNOW

orbit: the path of an object circling another object in space.

altitude: the height of an object above sea level.

How do rockets reach the heights and speeds they do? And how do they stay in space? After all, what goes up must come down, right? Even with the help of slingshots or catapults, every projectile you've ever launched eventually came back down to Earth.

Is it possible to get something moving so fast that it doesn't come back to Earth?

A CANNON ON A MOUNTAIN

Imagine climbing to the top of a very tall mountain, where the air is thin and cold. At the peak, you find a huge and powerful cannon, just waiting to be used. How far can this giant cannon fire?

First, you fire the cannon at its lowest setting, and watch as the cannonball disappears. The cannonball travels thousands of miles before it comes crashing back to Earth. That's good, but you want the cannonball to go farther. You increase the power of the cannon and try again.

This time, you hear reports that the cannon ball has traveled more than 12,000 miles—halfway around the world! Still not satisfied, you turn the cannon's power to maximum, and fire one more cannonball.

This time, there are no reports of the cannonball crashing to Earth. Nervously you wonder, where did it go?

Rockets use stages in different ways. **Check out how the Saturn V separated into many** stages on its way to the moon in this video!

(PS) YouTube Saturn V broke

The cannonball is traveling so quickly that even as gravity pulls it back to Earth, the earth's surface curves away from it. The cannonball is falling around the earth! This is called an **orbit**!

Welcome to Space!

Where does the atmosphere end and space begin? As you climb higher and higher, the air gradually becomes thinner and thinner. There's no exact line, and no sign that says, "Welcome to Space!" Scientists consider something to have entered space when it reaches an **altitude** of 62 miles above the surface of the earth. Does that seem high to you? It's 10 times higher than most passenger jets fly!

An orbit is the path an object takes around another object in space. In our solar system, planets, asteroids, and comets all orbit the sun, while natural satellites, or moons, orbit planets. Artificial satellites, such as the Hubble Space Telescope and the International Space Station, orbit the earth And some space probes even orbit other planets!

Getting into orbit isn't easy. First, a projectile must be traveling fast—at least 17,000 miles per hour. That's more than 10 times faster than a speeding bullet, and much faster than any cannon or rifle can fire a projectile.

Second, incredible speed isn't enough. When a projectile is moving that fast, the force of drag becomes very large! For an object to orbit the earth, it must be above the earth's atmosphere—in space. Otherwise, even the thinnest air will slow a satellite or spacecraft down, causing it to eventually fall on a ballistic trajectory back to the earth.

  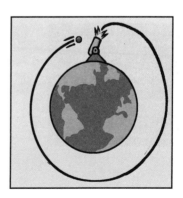

THE PATH OF A ROCKET

When a rocket is launched, it starts its flight pointing straight up. But as it accelerates, it begins to tip. This is normal! Just as with any projectile, a rocket needs a combination of horizontal and vertical motion to go as far and as fast as needed to get into orbit.

As its stages are left behind, the rocket becomes lighter and faster. After only a few minutes, the rocket's remaining engines shut down and the rocket has enough **momentum** to carry it into space. At this point, the rocket is on a ballistic trajectory. But a ballistic trajectory is a parabola, and that will bring it back to Earth! Instead, a rocket will fire its engines one more time, just long enough to change the shape of its path from a parabola to an **ellipse**. An ellipse is an oval shape. It's not perfectly round like a circle, but it's close.

At this point, the spacecraft is in orbit! And it will stay in orbit until another force acts to change its motion, just as Newton's first law says.

An artist's rendition of a space capsule re-entering Earth's atmosphere. That's a lot of friction!
credit: NASA

To come back to Earth, a spacecraft needs to slow down to change its path back from an ellipse to a parabola. **Retro-rockets** fire in the opposite direction of the spacecraft's motion, reducing its speed.

Once it enters the atmosphere, the spacecraft experiences a lot of drag. The friction between the air and the spacecraft is enough to heat the outside of the craft and the air around it to very high temperatures. Finally, the spacecraft is in freefall, once again acting like any other projectile, until its parachutes open to bring it down to a soft and safe landing.

Kepler

For centuries, astronomers believed that the moon and the planets all moved in perfect circles through the heavens. But in the seventeenth century, Dutch astronomer Johannes Kepler (1571–1630) proposed that their paths were not perfect circles, but ellipses. By carefully studying their motions, Kepler was able to use mathematics to determine his three laws of planetary motion, which are still used today.

BEYOND EARTH

Have you watched the *Apollo* astronauts hop around on the moon? Have you seen pictures of the *Curiosity* rover on Mars, or closeup shots of Jupiter's Great Red Spot? How did spacecraft get to Mars and Jupiter?

To leave Earth behind, a spacecraft needs to reach even greater speeds than what it needed to get into orbit. To escape the Earth's gravity completely, projectiles need to travel about 25,000 miles per hour. That's nearly 7 miles every second! This is called Earth's **escape velocity**. But even that isn't fast enough to travel to Mars or beyond.

DID YOU KNOW?

The temperatures on the outside of the *Apollo* spacecraft reached more than 5,000 degrees Fahrenheit (2,760 degrees Celsius) when it returned from the moon. Don't worry though—the astronauts were protected from that heat by a heatshield and were safe inside the cabin.

The farther you want to go, the faster you need to move.

The fastest spacecraft ever launched was the *New Horizons* space probe. It was sent on a trajectory toward Pluto at an incredible 36,000 miles per hour, and it still took more than nine years to reach its destination!

By observing everyday objects such as arrows and apples, scientists, including Galileo and Newton, showed that the laws that determined ballistic motion applied not only to things here at home, but to everything, everywhere. And you can, too! Every time you hit or kick a ball, shoot an arrow, or throw a pass, you're seeing the science of projectiles at work. From the smallest pebble shot with a slingshot to the biggest rocket sent into space, the study of projectiles can tell us a lot about the world around us, and even places beyond!

ESSENTIAL QUESTION

How are rockets similar to pebbles shot with a slingshot? How are they different?

TAKE FLIGHT

Have you ever wanted to build your own rocket and send it into space? The game Kerbal Space Program lets you build, test, and fly your own rockets through a series of challenges. Can you send your Kerbalnauts into orbit and bring them home safely? What about your own mission to the Mun, the large moon of Kerbal?

Note that this activity requires a paid service.

> **With an adult's permission,** try the game. Go to kerbaledu.com.

🔎 Kerbal Edu

Questions to think about

* Can you build a rocket with more than one stage?

* Are the game's laws of motion and gravity the same as they are in real life?

* How do control surfaces affect the flight of your rocket?

* How does using stages improve the flight of your rocket?

* Are you able to get to orbit or beyond?

* Does the game make spaceflight seem easy or hard?

> **You can also build airplanes in Kerbal Space Program.** Can you get one flying? Or get one into orbit?

> **There are many videos available** to help you get started, as well as in-game tutorials and help!

🔎 Kerbal game

Consider This!

How far can your rockets go? How many Kerbals can you launch at once and return safely?

LAUNCH TIME

You don't need a special launch pad or a million-dollar spacecraft to understand how rockets work. You can study their flight at home! All you'll need are supplies such as string, drinking straws, and balloons.

❯ **Attach one end of a piece of string to a sturdy object,** such as a chair or doorknob, or have friend or family member hold it.

❯ **Thread the string through one straw.** Attach the other end of the string to another sturdy object. Make sure the string is level and **taut**.

❯ **Blow up a balloon** and pinch the opening closed—don't tie it!

❯ **Attach the balloon to the straw** so that the balloon's opening points along the string.

❯ **Move the balloon and straw to one end of the string.** What do you think will happen when you release the balloon?

❯ **Release the balloon!** Write your observations and include a diagram in your engineering notebook.

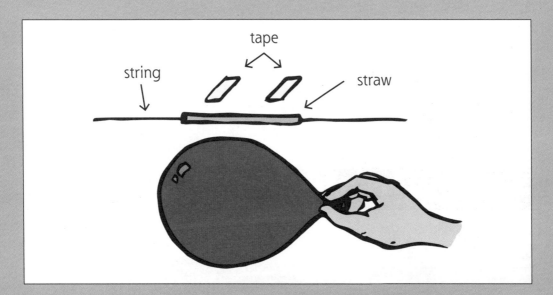

> **Vary the experiment by inflating the balloon with more air and then less air.** How does the amount of air affect the balloon's motion?

> **Now make the string vertical.** What happens when you release the balloon?

> **Keep your balloon setup** for another activity in this chapter!

Questions to think about

* What direction does the balloon travel when the string is horizontal? When it's vertical?

* Can you explain what's going on using Newton's laws?

* What forces affect the vertical launch more than the horizontal launch? Can you explain why?

Try This!

Try different sizes and shapes of balloons. What effect do size and shape have on the motion of the balloon? Is there a best size or shape to get the farthest distance? Think about the shape of rockets. Would making the balloon look more like a rocket change how far or fast it goes?

WORDS TO KNOW

taut: stretched tightly.

TO THE MOON!

Build your own liquid-fueled chemical rocket! While the fuels that real rockets use are extremely dangerous, you can use some common materials at home to get an idea of how these fuels work!

> **Caution:** Have an adult help you with this project, and do not perform this indoors! Use safety glasses.

> **Find a large, open space outside** to launch your rocket.

> **Place a cork inside the mouth of a plastic bottle** until you have a tight fit.

> **To make legs for the rocket,** securely tape three pencils equally spaced around the outside of the bottle at the mouth end. The cork should be about an inch from the ground.

> **Cut a sheet of paper towel in half.** Place a tablespoon of baking soda in the center of the paper towel.

> **Fold the paper towel** so that the baking soda doesn't fall out but can still fit through the bottle's mouth when it's time to add it.

> **Put on your safety glasses.**

> **Remove the cork** and pour about 1 to 2 inches of vinegar into your rocket.

> **Place the baking soda packet into the bottle,** and QUICKLY put the cork back in the bottle.

> **SHAKE the mixture for 2 to 3 seconds,** and then QUICKLY set the rocket down on its legs with the cork end facing down.

> **Stand back about 20 feet.** Watch it fly!

WORDS TO KNOW

ratio: the relationship in size or quantity between two things.

Questions to think about

* What happens when the baking soda meets the vinegar? Can you describe it in terms of potential and kinetic energy?

* How does the mixture cause the rocket to move?

* What other forces are working on the rocket as it moves?

Try This!

Try different amounts of vinegar and baking soda. Is there a **ratio** that works best? Try different sizes and shapes of bottles. How do they affect the rocket's flight? Can you describe the effect using the laws of motion? Can you improve the aerodynamics of your rocket?

Voyaging Voyagers

If an object is traveling with enough speed, it won't just leave Earth behind—it will leave the entire solar system! So far, only a few robotic spacecraft have managed this incredible feat. *Pioneers 10* and *11*, *Voyagers 1* and *2*, and *New Horizons* are all on trajectories out of our solar system and into interstellar space. Launched in 1977, *Voyager 1* is the manmade object farthest from Earth. In 40,000 years, it will pass the nearby star Gliese 445.

 You can track *Voyager 1*'s journey here.

Voyager 1 status

ON STAGE

How do stages help rockets travel farther and faster? To find out, you can make a two-stage rocket balloon!

❯ **Thread the string** from your first rocket balloon experiment (on page 108) through two plastic drinking straws. If you no longer have your rocket balloon track, turn back to the first experiment to set it up.

❯ **Cut a small ring** from a cardboard tube, about 1 inch wide.

❯ **Blow up one balloon** until it's about two-thirds full. It shouldn't be completely inflated.

❯ **Use a binder clip** to pinch the end closed or have an assistant hold it for you.

❯ **Without letting any air out,** pinch the first balloon's nozzle to the inside of the cardboard ring.

❯ **With its nozzle facing in the same direction** as the nozzle of the first balloon, pull a second balloon about one-third of the way through the cardboard tube.

❯ **Don't let the first balloon deflate!**

❯ **Inflate the second balloon** so that it pinches the nozzle of the first balloon inside the cardboard ring, keeping it from deflating. You might need someone to help you!

❯ **Pinch the nozzle** of the second balloon closed with a binder clip.

❯ **Tape each balloon** to one straw on the track.

❯ **Release the first balloon** to launch your two-stage balloon rocket! What happens?

Activity

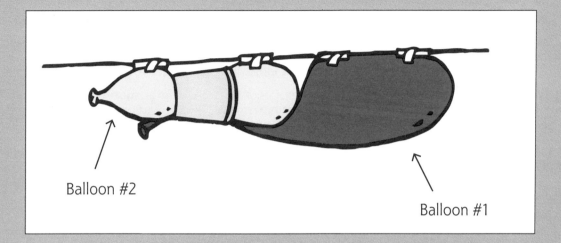

Balloon #2

Balloon #1

Questions to think about

* What's happening when you release the first balloon?

* Can you explain its motion using Newton's laws?

* What happens when the first balloon runs out of air?

* Do the balloons separate or stick together?

Try This!

Try taping the two balloons together so they don't separate when the first is deflated. How does that affect the speed and distance of the balloon rocket? Is it better to have them separate or stuck together? How do you think Isaac Newton would answer?

Try to add more stages! How far can your balloon rocket go?

Glossary

accelerate: to increase the speed of an object's movement.

action force: the force created by one object that acts upon another.

aerodynamic: having a shape that reduces the amount of drag created by air passing around or over it.

aeronautical engineer: a person who designs and tests aircraft.

air resistance: the force that acts on an object as it travels through the air.

altitude: the height of an object above sea level.

angle: the space between two lines that start from the same point, measured in degrees.

angular momentum: an object's resistance to either start or stop spinning due to inertia.

antenna: a metal rod that sends and receives radio waves. Plural is antennae.

artificial satellite: a man-made object that orbits the earth, moon, or other object.

astronomy: the study of the sun, moon, stars, planets, and space.

atlatl: a spear-thrower.

atmosphere: the mixture of gases surrounding Earth.

axis: an imaginary line down the middle of a sphere around which it rotates.

ballista: a large crossbow for firing a spear.

ballistic missile: a missile that is at first powered and guided but is then pulled by gravity to its target.

ballistics: the science that studies the movement of objects that are shot through the air.

ballistic trajectory: the trajectory of an object acted upon by only gravity and air resistance.

barrel: the straight shooting tube of a gun.

BCE: put after a date, BCE stands for Before Common Era and counts down to zero. CE stands for Common Era and counts up from zero. These non-religious terms correspond to BC and AD. This book was printed in 2018 CE.

biological warfare: the use of toxins or other biological matter as weapons.

booster: a rocket used to give another craft the power needed for takeoff.

bullet: the projectile used in guns.

buoyancy: the force that makes something able to float, either in the air or in the water.

calculus: a branch of mathematics involving calculations.

catapult: a large war machine used to hurl objects at an enemy.

chemical potential energy: energy that results from a chemical reaction.

combustion: a chemical reaction that produces heat and light.

combustion chamber: the part of a rocket where liquid fuel and oxidizer are combined to create a chemical reaction.

compound bow: a bow that uses a levering system, often cables and pulleys, to bend the limbs.

concentration camps: large camps where Jews and members of other groups were imprisoned by the Nazis during World War II. Prisoners were forced to perform hard labor and millions were killed.

contact force: a force that occurs when two objects are touching each other.

controversial: likely to cause the public to disagree and argue over something.

counterweight: a weight that balances another weight.

crossbow: a weapon used to shoot arrows.

culture: the beliefs and way of life of a group of people, which can include religion, language, art, clothing, food, holidays, tools, and more.

decelerate: to decrease the speed of an object's movement.

Glossary

deduction: a conclusion reached by reasoning or evidence.

drag: the force air exerts on a body moving through it.

ellipse: an oval shape.

energy: the ability or power to do things, to work.

engineer: a person who uses math, science, and creativity to solve problems or meet human needs.

escape velocity: the lowest velocity an object must have to escape the earth's gravitational pull.

exhaust: the hot gases produced from a rocket's engine.

fire lance: a very early gunpowder weapon.

fletching: feather-like material at the end of an arrow.

foe: an enemy.

force: a push or pull applied to an object.

fortification: a walled-in area to protect against an enemy.

free fall: when gravity is the only force acting on a moving object.

friction: a force that resists motion.

fulcrum: the point on which a lever rests or is supported and on which it pivots.

gravitational potential energy: the energy an object possesses because of its position in a gravitational field.

gravity: the force that pulls objects toward each other, and holds you on Earth.

gyroscope: a spinning wheel or disk used to measure or maintain orientation.

gyroscopic stabilization: when a spinning object stays pointed in the direction it was thrown.

horizontal: straight across from side to side.

hydrogen: a colorless, odorless, and flammable gas that is lighter than air.

independent: not influenced or affected by other things.

inertia: the resistance of an object to a change in its motion.

inversely: when something increases in relation to a decrease in another thing or vice versa.

jettison: to throw something away.

kinetic energy: energy associated with motion.

knuckleball: a baseball thrown with as little spin as possible.

lance: a long, straight wooden spear.

liquid-fueled rocket: a rocket that uses liquid propellants to create thrust.

liquid oxygen: a liquid produced by compressing oxygen gas.

lofted: an object that is propelled up.

longbow: a wooden bow drawn by hand.

machine: a device that transmits a force or motion.

Magnus effect: when air pressure on one side of a ball is greater than on the other side, making the ball move toward the side where there is less pressure.

mangonel: a military device for throwing stones and other projectiles.

marksman: a person aiming and shooting a weapon.

mass: a measure of the amount of matter in an object.

maximum height: when gravity slows the vertical velocity of a projectile to zero so it is neither rising nor falling.

maximum range: the greatest distance a projectile travels horizontally.

mechanical advantage: the amount a machine multiplies a force to make a task easier.

mechanical energy: energy that uses physical parts you can see, such as the parts of a machine. It is related to motion and height.

mechanics: the working parts of something.

Glossary

Middle Ages: the period of European history after the fall of the Roman Empire, from about 350 to 1450 CE.

missile: an object or weapon that is propelled toward a target.

momentum: the force that a moving object has in the direction that it is moving.

natural state: according to Aristotle, the way an object behaves when nothing is acting on it.

normal force: the support force pushing upward on an object from the ground.

optical illusion: a trick of the eyes that makes people see something differently than it really is.

orbit: the path of an object circling another object in space.

orientation: the direction and position of an object.

oxidizer: a substance that contains oxygen, which mixes with fuel in a rocket engine to help it burn.

parabola: an upside down, U-shaped curve that is a cross section of a cone.

parallel: two lines always the same distance apart.

payload: the object or load that is being delivered by the catapult.

perpendicular: a line at an angle of 90 degrees to another line or surface. The two lines form a corner, called a right angle.

physicist: a scientist who studies physical forces, including matter, energy, and motion, and how these forces interact with each other.

physics: the study of physical forces, including matter, energy, and motion, and how these forces interact with each other.

potential energy: energy that is stored.

prehistoric: having to do with ancient times, before written human records.

prey: an animal caught or hunted for food.

probe: a spaceship or other device used to explore outer space.

projectile: an object that is thrown or launched and does not move by its own power.

projectile motion: the path that a projectile takes as it travels.

projectile science: the study of how projectiles move.

propellant: a combination of fuel and oxidizer that burns to produce thrust in a rocket.

propel: to drive or move forward.

proportional: corresponding in size.

prototype: a model of something that allows engineers to test their idea.

pulley: a simple machine consisting of a wheel with a grooved rim that a rope or chain is pulled through to help lift a load.

radiation: energy transmitted in the form of rays, waves, or particles from a source, such as the sun.

range: the distance a projectile travels horizontally.

rate: the speed of something measured in an amount of time, such as miles per hour or feet per second.

ratio: the relationship in size or quantity between two things.

reaction force: the force acting in the opposite direction to the action force.

recoil: to spring back suddenly as the result of an action force.

recurve bow: a bow with limbs that curve away from the archer when unstrung.

retro-rocket: a rocket that is fired opposite the direction of motion to slow a spacecraft down.

siege: surrounding and attacking a fortified place, such as a fort, and cutting it off from help and supplies.

siege engine: a machine built to help forces break through walls— or go over them.

solar system: the collection of eight planets and their moons in orbit around the sun, together with smaller bodies in the form of asteroids, meteoroids, comets, and dwarf planets.

solid-fueled rocket: a rocket that uses solid propellants.

Glossary

Soviet Union: a country that existed from 1922 until 1991. Russia was part of the Soviet Union.

spear: a weapon with a long shaft and pointed tip, used for thrusting or throwing.

spear-thrower: a stick that makes it possible to throw spears farther and faster.

spiral: winding in a continuous and gradually widening or tightening curve.

stage: a smaller rocket that is stacked with other rockets and detaches when its fuel is used up.

streamlined: designed with a smooth surface that minimizes resistance through air or water

surface area: a measure of the total area that the surface of an object occupies.

taut: stretched tightly.

tension: a pulling force that pulls or stretches an object.

terminal velocity: the fastest an object will travel in free fall.

throttle: to control the amount of thrust.

thrust: a force that pushes an object forward.

torsion: a twisting force that turns or twirls a material.

trajectory: the curve a body travels along in its path through space.

trebuchet: a large, catapult-like structure with a moveable arm that launched damaging items into or over castle walls.

tundra: a treeless Arctic region that is permanently frozen below the top layer of soil.

turbulent: unsteady or violent movement.

variable: a symbol that holds the place for information that may change.

velocity: a measure of an object's speed and direction.

vertical: straight up and down.

warhead: a weapon that is the explosive part of a missile.

wary: suspicious.

work: a force that moves an object a distance.

Metric Conversions

Use this chart to find the metric equivalents to the English measurements in this book. If you need to know a half measurement, divide by two. If you need to know twice the measurement, multiply by two. How do you find a quarter measurement? How do you find three times the measurement?

English	Metric
1 inch	2.5 centimeters
1 foot	30.5 centimeters
1 yard	0.9 meter
1 mile	1.6 kilometers
1 pound	0.5 kilogram
1 teaspoon	5 milliliters
1 tablespoon	15 milliliters
1 cup	237 milliliters

Math Practice! (answers from page 38)

A football is kicked with a horizontal velocity of 22 feet per second and has a flight time of 2 seconds. How far did the football travel?
answer: 44 feet

A catapult flings a heavy boulder. It takes 5 seconds to reach its target with a horizontal velocity of 20 feet per second. How far away was the target?
answer: 100 feet

An arrow travels 200 feet. If its horizontal velocity was 50 feet per second, how long did it take to reach its target?
answer: 4 seconds

BOOKS

Gurstelle, William. *The Art of the Catapult: Build Greek Ballistae, Roman Onagers, English Trebuchets, and More Ancient Artillery.* Chicago Review Press, 2004.

Gurstelle, William. *Backyard Ballistics: Build Potato Cannons, Paper Match Rockets, Cincinnati Fire Kites, Tennis Ball Mortars, and More Dynamite Devices.* Chicago Review Press, 2012.

Mooney, Carla. *Rocketry: Investigate the Science and Technology of Rockets and Ballistics.* Nomad Press, 2014.

WEBSITES
NBC Learn: Check out the science of football!
nbclearn.com/science-of-nfl-football

WIRED: Check out the science behind the game Angry Birds
wired.com/2010/10/physics-of-angry-birds

Physics4Kids: Learn more about physics
physics4kids.com

NASA: Learn more about rocketry
nasa.gov/audience/foreducators/rocketry/home/index.html

University of Colorado, Boulder: Try these Phet Interactive Simulations
phet.colorado.edu/en/simulations/category/physics/motion

Resources

VIDEOS

SciShow videos on YouTube:
youtube.com/user/scishow

Veritasium videos on YouTube:
youtube.com/user/1Veritasium/feed

QR CODE GLOSSARY

page 6: *youtube.com/watch?v=1KVesnLv_mc*

page 8: *freeangrybirdsgame.org/play/angry_birds_online.html*

page 10: *youtube.com/watch?v=aJc4DEkSq4I*

page 20: *exploratorium.edu/ronh/weight*

page 21: *youtube.com/watch?v=KlWpFLfLFBI*

page 26: *leaningtowerpisa.com/facts/why/why-pisa-leaning-tower-does-not-fall*

page 27: *youtube.com/watch?v=E43-CfukEgs*

page 33: *youtube.com/watch?v=urQCmMiHKQk*

page 37: *m.mlb.com/glossary/statcast/projected-home-run-distance*

page 38: *phet.colorado.edu/sims/html/projectile-motion/latest/projectile-motion_en.html*

page 40: *si.com/mlb/2018/03/22/wil-myers-launch-angle*

page 45: *youtube.com/watch?v=uRijc-AN-F0*

page 54: *phet.colorado.edu/sims/html/energy-skate-park-basics/latest/energy-skate-park-basics_en.html*

page 56: *historic-uk.com/HistoryUK/HistoryofEngland/Robin-Hood*

page 58: *vimeo.com/45555883*

page 61: *youtube.com/watch?v=yi4p8ZR4n28*

page 63: *youtube.com/watch?v=sXuQvAPwcOE*

page 64: *youtube.com/watch?v=gLVQE2Ml9z8*

page 67: *youtube.com/watch?v=IQbK6kdTtHg*

page 76: *solarsystem.nasa.gov/resources/329/the-apollo-15-hammer-feather-drop*

page 79: *ted.com/talks/alan_eustace_i_leapt_from_the_stratosphere_here_s_how_i_did_it#t-57289*

page 79: *theguardian.com/us-news/2014/oct/25/google-executive-alan-eustace-beats-felix-baumgartners-skydiving-record*

page 81: *youtube.com/watch?v=YIPO3W081Hw*

QR CODE GLOSSARY (Continued)

page 82: *youtube.com/watch?v=6R-cF-5CciE*

page 84: *youtube.com/watch?v=cquvA_lpEsA*

page 95: *youtube.com/watch?v=9KnIqblQEeM*

page 97: *youtube.com/watch?v=sB_nEtZxPog*

page 98: *space.com/18422-apollo-saturn-v-moon-rocket-nasa-infographic.html*

page 100: *youtube.com/watch?v=2aCOyOvOw5c*

page 100: *youtube.com/watch?v=A0FZIwabctw*

page 102: *youtube.com/watch?v=_Kq67RcfSpw*

page 107: *kerbaledu.com*

page 107: *youtube.com/playlist?list=PLYu7z3I8tdEm5nyZU3a-O2ak6mBYXWPAL*

page 111: *voyager.jpl.nasa.gov/mission/status*

ESSENTIAL QUESTIONS

Introduction: Why did ancient humans develop methods of sending projectiles farther, faster? How did this ability make life better?

Chapter 1: What are the different forces that control movement, and what would life be like without these forces?

Chapter 2: When might it be useful to know the height and distance a projectile has traveled?

Chapter 3: Why do people keep inventing new and improved ways of sending projectiles through the air?

Chapter 4: What are some different ways of manipulating the motion of a projectile through the air, and why are these useful?

Chapter 5: How are rockets similar to pebbles shot with a slingshot? How are they different?

Index